FROM EGYPT TO THE PROMISED LAND

From Egypt to the Promised Land by Karen Roper
Published by Karen Roper ©

The moral right of the author has been asserted. All rights reserved. Without limiting the rights under copyright restricted above, no part of this publication may be reproduced, stored in or introduced into a retrieval system, or transmitted, in any form or by any means (electronic, mechanical, photocopying, recording or otherwise), without the prior written permission of the copyright owner.

1st Edition 2022, pbk.
ISBN: 978-0-6455581-0-4
Designer: Amanda Greenslade, typeset in Nassim Latin 12/14

www.livingthelifegodintended.com

All quotations from the Bible are from the

Spirit Filled Life Bible Copyright © 1991 by Thomas Nelson, Inc.

From Egypt to the Promised Land

A walk through the Christian journey

Karen Roper

Table of Contents

Prologue—The Journey	7
Chapter 1—Our Salvation	11
Chapter 2—Our First Steps With God	21
Chapter 3—Our Baptism	31
Chapter 4—The Wilderness: Provision	41
Chapter 5— The Wilderness: Worship and Unity	53
Chapter 6—The Wilderness: Our Covenant	65
Chapter 7—The Wilderness: Our Priesthood	75
Chapter 8—The Wilderness: The Battle for Trust in God	85
Chapter 9—The Wilderness: The Battle of Leading	105
Chapter 10—The Wilderness: The Battle of Emotions	127
Chapter 11—Review of Lessons Learned	147
Chapter 12—The Jordan River	181
Epilogue	193

Prologue—The Journey

Have you ever been on a long journey either by plane, bus or car? I have and it seems to take forever sometimes. My boy's favourite saying on a long car journey (more than 30 minutes) was 'Are we there yet?'

Sometimes we're so impatient to end the journey that if we're travelling by car or bus, we miss the scenery as we go by. We don't take time to enjoy the differing landscapes or the quaint little towns we pass through.

One of the camping trips that we took as a family was like this. We kept driving for a day and a half. We stopped overnight and for lunches and breaks, but we didn't really see any of the towns we passed through. We didn't stop to learn anything about the history or see any of the interesting sights. We just drove.

For many of us, it seems like the destination is far more important than the journey there. Maybe it's because many hours were spent in preparation just to get on the road. It seems like forever since we started planning and we're impatient to get there.

This is what it's like for many of us in our Christian walk. We come to know Jesus as our Saviour and we want all the blessings that come from that to happen in an instant. If you haven't noticed, God is not an 'instant' God. For God, the journey is just as important as the destination, for it's on that journey that we learn to trust God, to rely on Him and to make Him Lord and not just Saviour.

Another of our family camping journeys was different.

Every time we came to a new town, we took out the guidebook to see if anything was interesting in the town. We went through historical museums and old butter factories, ate the local produce and had a good time exploring those towns on the way to our destination.

Being a Christian is like this. There are new experiences for us to enjoy or just get through, new things to learn, new revelations about who God is and that is just the beginning. Because of this, God can only change us on the journey. He can't change us if we sit at the foot of the cross and just accept Him as our Saviour. Likewise, He can't change us if He gives us everything we need in an instant. Sometimes that happens and it's called a miracle, but most often this is not what happens.

We must take the journey to renew our minds to line up with God's Word. In other words, change our thinking so we think like God.

In Romans 12:2, it states:

> *And do not be conformed to this world, but be transformed by the renewing of your mind, that you may prove what is that good and acceptable and perfect will of God.*

This is how the journey changes us.

Through this book we'll look at the different changes and experiences we can allow ourselves to go through (it's still our choice, but the results will be worth it). For a lot of us, when we go through our Christian walk we struggle with many issues. Many things also come out of our hearts and through our mouths. We're never sure why they come up.

There's a story in the Bible that will help us through those things and that is the journey from Egypt to the Promised Land. We don't take this journey just once in our lifetime, but continually, as God takes us through the process of becoming more like Jesus.

God is changing us from glory to glory and most always does it this way. Sometimes miracles happen and things in our lives are removed in an instant but in most cases, God wants us to take the journey. Why? In the journey, we learn to love God and trust Him more. It's a journey that will shape our character and integrity.

As we go through this journey together, we'll ask God to make that journey with us. It's only through His strength and provision that we will make it.

So let's begin.

You and I are now in the shoes of the Israelites. They made the journey in the natural; we will make it in the spiritual. However, we'll use their example to help us in our spiritual walk with God.

Let's pray before we start:

> *Lord, we come to you and ask that you take us on this journey. We don't want to be stagnant in our walk with you. We want to keep growing so we can become more like Jesus. We want to walk in your will and your plan for our lives so help us grow as we take this journey together. Amen.*

Chapter 1—Our Salvation

The first step on our Christian journey is the moment we decide to make Jesus our Saviour and more importantly, our Lord. If He's only our Saviour, we'll only make it to the Red Sea, but if we make Him our Lord, He promises to lead and guide us through every step to the Promised Land (Psalm 23:2-3).

We might backtrack a moment and find out the reason we need a Saviour. It goes back to the book of Genesis and the Garden of Eden. God created man and woman perfect and all went well for a while. But something happened. It sounds like a movie plot—it all starts well, then something bad happens and then there's a happily ever after.

Satan came along and tempted Eve, then Adam, with the promise they could be like God. They ate the fruit and then their eyes were opened, and they knew good and evil. Prior to that, all they had known was good things and the blessing of God. God banned them from the garden and then they lost their relationship with God on a spiritual level. No longer were they clothed with the glory of God, but with animal skins. They could talk to God but no longer would they walk intimately with Him daily. Instead, they hid from God in shame. This curse (sin nature) was passed on to all humankind because they were the first physical parents.

This was the same for all God's people in the Old Testament. The relationship between them and God had been destroyed. God spoke to people in the Old Testament, but it was mainly to the prophets and those who sought God with all their hearts.

The Israelites knew God by ritual and law until Jesus came.

Because Jesus took our sin on the cross and bore that curse for us, we were restored to God spiritually (God now lives in us). But this time, it's our choice to believe. If we believe, we're restored to relationship and grace. The curse hangs over all those who still don't believe.

Now back to our story. This was the same as the Israelites living in Egypt. God promised Joseph that they would live there for 430 years and then they would return to the land God had promised Abraham, Isaac and Jacob. I find it interesting that the Israelites were crying out about their situation to God but nobody was praying that the promise would come to pass Exodus 3:7). There seemed to be nobody with a relationship with God that He could communicate the promise through.

When the Israelites were taken captive from Jerusalem (many years later) and forced to live in Babylon, the same type of promise was given. They were told by the prophets, prior to the time of captivity, that they would live in captivity in Babylon for 70 years. After the Israelites had gone into captivity, Daniel discovered this promise (Daniel 9:2 -3) and started to pray about it instead of complaining to God.

Physical salvation for the Israelites

Let's look at the physical saving (salvation) from Egypt for the Israelites. For saving to occur, there must be some sort of rescue. In the Pocket Oxford Dictionary, 'save' means to rescue or preserve from danger, harm or discredit. For example, if we're in the ocean and can't swim, we put our hands up and the lifesavers come to rescue us.

God began the rescue of the Israelites from Egypt when He heard their cries. In Exodus 3:7–8a, God told Moses:

> *"I have surely seen the oppression of My people who are in Egypt, and have heard their cry because of their taskmasters, for I know their sorrows. So I have come down to deliver them out of the hand of the Egyptians and to bring them up from that land to a good and large land."*

God always speaks His Word before the promises come to pass. Once God speaks, He expects that what He says will come to pass. That's how creation happened—God spoke and what He spoke happened. It's necessary to remind ourselves that with God, there is no time. We are held to time but God is not.

It's interesting to note that although the Israelites weren't praying regarding the promise God had given to Abraham many years before, regarding their time in Egypt (Genesis 15:13-14), God always keeps His promises regardless. God also provides a way to make them come to pass. Therefore, God started the deliverance (saving) of His people from that moment on.

However, God always requires a person to deliver His promise. The person God chose was Moses (verse 10). God will generally minister through a person for your salvation as well, although in some cases, God can appear to you in dreams and visions (like the Apostle Paul when Jesus appeared to him on the road to Damascus in the book of Acts).

After that happens, there is still a 'doing' on our part. Romans 10:9 tells us what our part is:

> *That if you confess with your mouth the Lord Jesus and believe in your heart that God has raised Him from the dead, you will be saved.*

The 'doing' part for us is always confession and believing. This is a principle of God that we will continually refer to throughout this book. It doesn't only relate to salvation but relates to other promises and blessings that God wants to give us.

What happens when we get saved (after we have confessed and believed)? There's a beautiful explanation of this in the book of Zechariah 3:3–5a, which states:

> *Now Joshua was clothed with filthy garments and was standing before the Angel. Then He answered and spoke to those who stood before Him, saying, "Take away the filthy garment from him." And to him He said, "See, I have removed your iniquity from you, and I will clothe you with rich robes." And I said, "Let them put a clean turban on his head." So they put a clean turban on his head, and they put the clothes on him.*

This is what happens to us when we're saved. Jesus removes our sins as far as the east is from the west and remembers them no more, then He clothes us with robes of righteousness (which signifies right standing with God).

The next step is to take the journey. Once the lifesaver has reached you in the ocean, a journey to the shore must be undertaken. You can't do it on your own; you must follow the lifesaver's instructions and allow him to guide you.

This is what happened to the Israelites. Moses returned to Egypt and told them that God had seen their misery and was going to save them. The Israelites believed Moses and they all rejoiced by bowing their heads and worshipping God (Exodus 4:31). Their journey towards freedom had commenced.

However, things became bad before God delivered them. First, Moses and Aaron went to Pharaoh and told him to let all the Israelites go on a three-day journey into the wilderness to sacrifice to God (Exodus 5:3). But of course, Pharaoh wouldn't let the Israelites go without a fight and that can happen to us as well. We can go to church, youth group or Sunday school and hear the Bible taught to us, but an enemy is trying to stop that Word from becoming personal to us. This is because there's always an enemy fighting against God.

What happened to the Israelites? Pharaoh made them work harder than they ever had before. Has that happened to you? You might have believed that God wanted to save you and that He loved you, but after giving your heart to Jesus, bad things started to happen.

Once we hear the Word of God and want to follow Him, Satan tries to get us to believe that it never happened—that we can still live the way we want to and God didn't mean it. This isn't true and we need to know that once we give our lives to God, we're in His Kingdom. We can't let Satan steal the Word of God from our hearts. In Mark 4:14–15, it says:

> *The sower sows the word, and these are the ones by the wayside where the word is sown. When they hear, Satan comes immediately and takes away the word that was sown in their hearts.*

We need to instead believe the promise of God in Romans 10:9, which states:

> *That if you confess with your mouth the Lord Jesus and believe in your heart that God has raised Him from the dead, you will be saved.*

But God had a plan to deliver the Israelites and He does for us too. God worked a number of miracles in Egypt which proved that the Egyptian gods weren't powerful or strong and God was stronger than them. Let's take a look at those miracles in groups.

Miracles showing the power of God and the Egyptian enchanters

The first two miracles that Moses performed were also performed by the Egyptian enchanters. The effects of these miracles were felt by the Israelites and the Egyptians. This seems strange until we reflect on our own journey after salvation.

These miracles were turning the waters of the Nile River into blood and the plague of frogs (Exodus 7 and 8). Both the Egyptians and the Israelites suffered throughout these two plagues. God didn't miraculously save the Israelites from what was going on.

This can happen on our journey after salvation. The things happening in the world can affect everyone. But unlike everyone else in the world, what's our response when bad things happen, especially so soon after salvation? Are we still going to trust in God and believe that He's good or are we going to lose our trust in God quickly?

It reminds me of the scripture in Mark 4:16–17 where the Word of God is sown and then salvation is received gladly. A short time later, bad things happen and we doubt our salvation and then it seems to be snatched away from us. Jesus said we will have trials but 'take heart (or trust Me), I have overcome them'.

So, after salvation, if this has happened to you a long time ago or is happening now, trust God. He has a good plan for your life and wants to build up your trust in Him.

Miracles showing the power of God only

The next miracle that Moses performed couldn't be reproduced by the Egyptian enchanters. Even the Egyptian enchanters said, 'It is the finger of God' (Exodus 8:19).

God was starting to show the Egyptians the distinction between Him and their gods.

Miracles showing the power of God and the separation of the Israelites

The next six miracles that Moses performed (which the Egyptian enchanters couldn't) didn't affect the Israelites at all (Exodus 8:22). God was starting to show the Egyptians the distinction between them and the Israelites.

The Israelites were dwelling under God's favour and protection as His people. This is how God wants us to live in this world—not separated from it but abiding in Him and living and dwelling under His favour and protection.

By the time the first nine miracles had been undertaken, the land of Egypt had been ravaged and destroyed, but still Pharaoh hardened his heart and wouldn't let the Israelites go.

There's a lesson for us here too. We need to heed the Word of God and stay under His favour and protection and not harden our hearts. God said that 'obedience is better than sacrifice'. We can do a lot of Christian things for God but if we don't obey, then we have hardened our hearts to what God wants to accomplish in and through us.

The last plague

The last plague that came upon the Egyptians (because Pharaoh had hardened his heart) was the death of the firstborn son in every Egyptian family (Exodus 11:5). This plague instituted the Passover for the Israelites, which resulted in Communion for the Christians.

For the Egyptians, this signalled the end of the plagues and the exodus of the Israelites, who had been their slaves. For the Israelites, this last plague became a remembrance of what God had done for them on this night (the institution of the Passover).

But unlike the other plagues, the Israelites weren't guaranteed God's favour and protection. This time they had to do something to prevent them from suffering the same fate as the Egyptians. The Israelites had to take a perfect lamb and kill it at twilight on a certain day. They then had to smear its blood on the doorposts and lintel of their houses. They had to all stay inside their houses and eat the lamb and unleavened bread with their families, fully clothed and prepared for what God had in store for them next. When the death angel, saw the blood on the doors and lintels, he passed over that house. This was their salvation—the choice they had to make to follow God or not.

For us, there's a moment we can choose salvation too. When Jesus died on the cross, He became the Passover lamb, so that whoever chooses to believe in Him can be saved.

The Israelites remember the night they escaped from the Egyptians as Passover. The Christians remember the night Jesus died by partaking in Communion.

Could the Israelites have lost that salvation? Yes, they could have if they hadn't obeyed God and put the blood on the doorposts and lintels, or if they had walked outside when the angel of death was passing over or if they hadn't obeyed God's instructions to eat the lamb and the unleavened bread. Their fate would have been the same as the Egyptians.

What about us? Can we lose our salvation? Yes, I believe we can. Once we're saved, we're not always saved (Hebrews 6:4-5). It's not good for us to want what the world has to offer. It may look more appealing on the outside, but if you go back to the way of the world, you may pay a high price. Jesus can redeem you again if you repent, but this time the obstacle of guilt and shame can sometimes appear too high. You're lost in your sin and now there's a contention with the guilt of rejecting Jesus already to contend with (Hebrews 6:6). But if you make the first move by repenting, God will welcome you back.

The Exodus

After that last plague, Pharaoh agreed to let the people go, including all their possessions. The Israelites then asked the Egyptians for articles of silver, gold and clothing which they agreed to and gave them. Therefore, they plundered the Egyptians and came out, not as slaves, but prosperous in possessions.

The Israelites also went out in health from the oldest down to the youngest as there was no one feeble among them (Psalm 105:37). Feeble, in this context, means to totter or waver (Strongs

Exhaustive Concordance of the Bible). None of them were stumbling or shaking, which means they were walking strong. By God's mercy and grace, they must have been supernaturally healed of their injuries from the Egyptians' whips and other illnesses they had.

Once we are saved, all God's blessings are given to us and we become joint-heirs with Jesus to all God's blessings. Unlike the Israelites, we need to believe and confess these promises until they come to pass in our lives. But as far as God is concerned, the moment we are saved, we are also healed, delivered, set free and prospering in our spirit, soul and body.

The journey we're about to undertake will instruct you on how to receive these blessings over your life and more importantly, keep them. We don't want only a miracle of finances, we want to live financially prosperous. Likewise, we don't want a miracle of healing, we want to live in divine health.

So as we start to take this journey, let's pray:

> *Father, we thank you that you have saved us and we now live in the Kingdom of light. We thank you for all of your promises in Your Word and we want to obey and live them all. Please help us as we take this journey to understand Your Word and You more so that we can live the abundant life that You came to give us. In Jesus' name, amen.*

Chapter 2—Our First Steps With God

When we first give our lives to Jesus, we believe everything in our lives from then on will be easier. This happens for a while—some of our prayers may be answered quickly and blessings come into our lives. We're on fire for God and tell everyone about Him. Sunday mornings can't come quick enough as we want to be in church singing the praises of God and hearing the message—a new revelation of God. Reading the Bible and praying (talking to God) are things we want to do all the time.

It seems like our life is just about perfect and then reality hits. Why is this? Did we do something to jeopardise our salvation or did we upset God in some way? We can feel like a baby who's just started to walk. Now our parents want us to walk everywhere and not be carried all the time. If we'd known that, we wouldn't have walked … or would we?

Just as babies must go through the development stages to become toddlers, then children, teenagers and on to adults, God expects us to spiritually grow in Him. Ephesians 4:14–15 says:

> *That we should no longer be children, tossed to and fro and carried about with every wind of doctrine, by the trickery of men, in the cunning craftiness of deceitful plotting, but, speaking the truth in love, may grow up in all things into Him who is the head—Christ.*

We then need to have our minds renewed to the way God thinks, as in Romans 12:2:

> *And do not be conformed to this world, but be transformed by the renewing of your mind, that you may prove what is that good and acceptable and perfect will of God.*

This is what the Israelites went through after they came out of Egypt. In Exodus 13:17, it states that God did not lead them on a direct path to the Promised Land but led the people by way of the wilderness so they would not see war and want to return to Egypt.

If the Israelites had experienced war with the nations this early on in the way to the Promised Land, then they might not have wanted to continue but would certainly have desired to go back to Egypt. This is the reason that once we are saved, everything seems to go right for a time. God doesn't want us to return to Egypt (our old way of life) but wants us to continue with Him. So he leads us gently, like He did the Israelites.

The first thing the Israelites experienced when they started out was God's immediate protection of them. In Exodus 13: 21–22 it states:

> *And the Lord went before them by day in a pillar of cloud to lead the way, and by night in a pillar of fire to give them light, so as to go by day and night. He did not take away the pillar of cloud by day or the pillar of fire by night from before the people.*

God immediately protected the Israelites in two different ways, which covered them 24 hours a day, seven days a week. The wilderness was a hot place by day and a cold place at night.

The pillar of cloud used by God during the day was likely to shade them from the extreme heat of the desert. This meant that the Israelites could keep walking all day if necessary. The little ones and the elderly would not get heatstroke. As I sit here writing, my town has just been through a five-day heatwave, with another on the way later in the week. The humidity was oppressive and we needed to drink lots of water. Normally, I don't feel the high temperatures as much because the cool sea breeze arrives around noon and cools the place down. This time, there was no cool sea breeze, just a hot wind. It was stifling. Just like this, God protected His people by providing them with that cloud.

The pillar of fire used by God during the night was to provide light, as the verse mentions, but it was also likely used to keep the Israelites warm. If God needed them to walk through the night, they could because of the light but if He required them to camp for the night, they could as they would be warm.

God provides for our protection too. When we're saved, it's through the blood of Jesus. When Jesus died on the cross, His blood was poured out not only for our sin but also for our protection.

Our protection comes the same way it did when the Israelites put the blood of the slain lamb on their doorposts and lintels. God requires that we do the same thing but in a spiritual sense. This requires us to believe that what Jesus did for us is true and say that out loud (for example, 'I plead the blood of Jesus over me').

Believing comes first because this is our faith in action. In Hebrews 11:6, it states that it is impossible to please God without faith. Faith is believing something will come to pass before we see it. It's a lot like the day before we get paid. We have faith that we will be paid the next day. We can't see it but we know in our hearts that it's going to happen.

My favourite scripture for believing God for my protection is found in Psalm 91. This Psalm in my Bible is titled 'Safety of Abiding in the Presence of God'. The first verse tells us that we can only be safe if we dwell in the secret place of the Most High. Where is that secret place? That secret place comes when we continually walk with God daily.

In John 15, it states that He is the vine and we are the branches. We need to be continually connected to the vine to stay safe. So what does that look like? It means listening for and to the voice of the Holy Spirit giving you direction in your life. Every day Jesus received His orders from God. We should too and that's how close we should be. In the busyness of our lives, sometimes we don't do it, but God protects us anyway because He loves us. But we need to get back on track and abide with Him.

The rest of the psalm tells us what God will deliver us from. Now we've found our promise of protection, what's next? We need to confess it. Confessing means speaking it with your mouth so it gets down to your heart and you not only believe it, but it becomes the only truth. So when you are confronted with a situation where you need God's protection, that psalm comes from your heart into your mouth and you speak it without even thinking about it. The power to overcome situations is always found in the Word of God.

In my life, for protection (as well as believing and confessing the Word of God), I plead the blood of Jesus over my house, my family, my workplace and every place we walk through nearly every single day. It's similar to what the Israelites did in Egypt when they put the blood of the lamb on the doorposts and lintel of their houses to protect everyone inside. I will only know when I get to heaven how much the blood of Jesus has protected me, my family and my possessions.

The second thing the Israelites experienced was that the enemy is real. Most of the time, we, as Christians, forget that an enemy is fighting against us. The Bible states in Ephesians 6:12 that 'we do not fight [wrestle] against flesh and blood [people and their ideas and opinions] but we fight against principalities, powers, the rulers of the darkness of this age and spiritual hosts of wickedness in the heavenly places.' There is a war and it's in the spiritual realm, not the natural realm.

The Israelites experienced an attack from the enemy soon after they were delivered. You would think that once we're saved, we can sit back and put our feet up. It might work that way for a while, but an attack is imminent. In 1 Peter 4:12, it states that we should not think it strange or be surprised at the fiery trial that has come to try us but we need to rejoice in the fact that we can partake in Christ's sufferings.

What did Jesus suffer when He was on the earth? The first thing was temptation by Satan in Matthew 4. How did Jesus conquer the enemy? By quoting the Word of God back at Satan.

Jesus also suffered persecution from the Pharisees and other religious leaders. How did He conquer the enemy (not the people, but the tempter behind them)? In many different ways—He healed the sick, He wrote on the ground, He used wisdom and many other things. How did He know what to use? God told Him.

What enemy did the Israelites first experience? It was the one they'd been delivered from—the Egyptians. Oftentimes the thing that comes back to tempt us after we're saved is what we were delivered from. If you had an alcohol addiction, it may be that. If you had a nasty way of talking to people, it may be that. If, like me, you had an anger issue, it may be that. The good news is that we don't have to succumb to the enemy's attacks.

Let's see what the Israelites did. The Israelites didn't know the enemy was coming until it drew near (Exodus 14:10). Their first reaction was to be afraid, cry out to the Lord and blame God and Moses for their predicament.

As they were newly delivered, Moses didn't rebuke them for their complaining and blaming, but spoke what God told him. In verses 13 and 14, Moses says:

> *"Do not be afraid. Stand still, and see the salvation of the Lord, which He will accomplish for you today. For the Egyptians, whom you see today, you shall see again no more forever. The Lord will fight for you, and you shall hold your peace."*

The first thing Moses told them was not to be afraid. The only way we cannot be afraid in most situations is by trusting in God. We need to recognise that God doesn't give us fear, He gives us peace, if we will trust Him. 2 Timothy 1:7 reminds us that 'God has not given us a spirit of fear, but of power, of love and of a sound mind.' We have the power in God to overcome, we have the love of God to overcome and we have a sound mind to make wise decisions and speak the Word of God. We need not fear.

It's hard to do this until we've built up our trust level in God in each area of our lives. Recently, in my life, certain situations caused me to feel overwhelmed and burnt out. Instead of running to God before I burnt out, I waited until later. By then, the spirit of fear had overtaken me and I needed to run back to God and confess the Word until my trust level was again built up and I knew He would never leave me or forsake me. All of us go through it, at different levels. But the Word of God is powerful and will defeat any attack from the enemy.

The second thing Moses told them was to 'stand still'. Often, when the enemy comes against us, all we want to do is run. But the only way the enemy will know we're serious is if we stand still. Ephesians 6:10–18 teaches us about the armour of God that we have at our disposal. I encourage you to read all those verses but verse 13 is the one I want to concentrate on:

> *Therefore take up the whole armor of God, that*
> *you may be able to withstand in the evil day,*
> *and having done all, to stand.*

This is our position in God when the enemy comes—to stand. In the Oxford dictionary, 'stand' means to 'be in a stationary, upright position, rise to it from lying or sitting or kneeling or be situated and hold position'. I love the last part of that definition. 'Be situated and hold position' infers that we're ready and we know who we are in God and whose we are. We're holding our position and standing on the Word of God until the enemy leaves. We don't defeat him—Jesus had already done this—we just have to stand our ground no matter how hard it is or how long it takes.

James 4:7 tells us:

> *Therefore, submit to God. Resist the devil and*
> *he will flee from you.*

The only way we can resist the devil is by staying under the blood covering of Jesus and standing on the Word of God. That verse reminds us that the enemy will flee. So if you're in a battle, keep standing and you will see victory.

The third thing that Moses told them was 'to see the salvation of the Lord'. We need to be continually seeing with our spiritual eyes that the Word will work. Salvation means deliverance, help or welfare. We need to see it before we experience it. That is called faith.

The last thing that Moses told them was that they would see the enemy no more. But, you say, didn't the Israelites continue to have trials? That's right, they did. It's important to realise that this was the first enemy they encountered after they left Egypt. Other enemies were waiting for them. However, the first one is always the hardest. After the first one is defeated, you know God can stand with you to defeat all the enemies that come against you.

Did the Israelites see the Egyptians anymore? No, they didn't. What was the reason? The Lord fought for them as the Israelites held their peace and did not fear. This is a key for us too. The Lord will only fight for us when we have no fear but complete trust in him.

As I have stated previously, the Lord provides for our protection. Even though the Egyptians were coming toward the Israelites, they did not come near them. In verses 19 and 20 of chapter 14, we read that the Angel of the Lord went behind the Israelites. This resulted in the Israelite camp having light and the Egyptian camp being in darkness. When God is with us, there is always light. God is light and darkness cannot be near Him. I love what verse 20 says: 'so that the one side did not come near the other all that night'. The Israelites could go to the Egyptians because they had the light but the Egyptians were in darkness and could not go to the Israelites.

The light in the Israelite camp also assured them that God was with them even in dire circumstances. Psalm 23 tells us that 'though I walk through the valley of the shadow of death, I will fear no evil: For You are with me: Your rod and Your staff, they comfort me.' Even though we feel like the enemy's attack is too strong and we won't make it, God promises us that He will walk us through. We don't camp in the attack, we walk through the attack.

Another promise from God is that He will never leave us or forsake us (Hebrews 13:5). Sometimes, we leave God because we want to walk our own path. When we come back onto the path of God, He is waiting for us—He never left, He's just waiting for us to rejoin Him. The Israelites knew God was with them so they did not fear.

The next thing the Israelites had to do was 'go forward'. They couldn't camp on that side of the Red Sea. For the promise of God to come to pass, they had to keep moving forward. The Red Sea was in front of them and the enemy behind. It looked like an impossible situation for deliverance to occur. But God is the God of the impossible. God can only make Himself known in our lives through those situations that seem impossible. When you're facing those types of situations and come through them with peace and joy, others will ask you how you did it. It's only God who brings us through because there are no answers in the natural.

For the Israelites to go forward, they had to walk through the Red Sea. We'll cover the meaning of that in the next chapter. For now, let's pray and thank God for His protection, His assurance and our position in Him before we, like the Israelites, move forward.

Father, we thank you that You are our God, You are our protector and we can have assurance because You are beside us. Lord, as we make the next step in our journey, please continue to be with us, helping us become more like Jesus and growing closer to you. Amen!

Before we go to the next chapter, we need to remember to take with us what we've already learnt. Let's take a moment to recap. We've learnt that God is our Saviour so we have given our lives to Him and that God is our Lord so we can trust Him always. We've learnt that God is our protector and He is our peace. We know that we have an enemy but with God, we're overcomers. Are you ready for the next stage of this journey?

Chapter 3—Our Baptism

For all of us, there comes a time in our Christian walk where we must make a firm decision to follow Jesus, no matter what comes. When we have made that decision, we undergo what is called baptism. Baptism is different from christening. Your parents may have christened you as a child and dedicated you to the Lord. Baptism is not your parents' decision, it's yours—to forsake all and follow Christ. It happens when we're much older in years than we are when we are christened (dedicated to the Lord).

On the Israelites' journey to the Promised Land, they underwent a baptism. The enemy was chasing them and the only way to defeat them was to go through the Red Sea. Let's pick the story up in Exodus 14:21 and 22:

> *Then Moses stretched out his hand over the sea; and the Lord caused the sea to go back by a strong east wind all that night, and made the sea into dry land, and the waters were divided. So the children of Israel went into the midst of the sea on the dry ground, and the waters were a wall to them on their right hand and on their left.*

The parting of the Red Sea is an exciting miracle that God performed. Think about it. You're one of the Israelites. You know the enemy is chasing you and Moses has told you not to be afraid, that God is going to deliver you. You watch in awe as Moses stretches out his hand over the Red Sea. The waters start to go back and dry land starts to appear. You can't believe your eyes. Then Moses tells you to start walking. As your feet first touch that sea bed, you expect it to be soggy and wet, however, it's totally dry.

You keep walking through, on the one hand, worried that the wall of water on each side might come crashing down and on the other, amazed. You might even see fish and other marine creatures swimming in the water.

You reach the other side and turn around. You watch in horror as the enemy starts to make their way across the dry sea bed. Oh no! You thought you were safe. Then Moses again holds out his hand and the sea comes back on the enemy and they're all drowned. A sigh of relief comes to you and then immense gratitude to God for saving you. You'll never forget this day ... or will you? We'll find out in the next chapter.

That's not the only miracle God performed that day. In verse 31 of Chapter 14, it tells us of the Israelites' reaction:

> *Thus Israel saw the great work which the Lord*
> *had done in Egypt; so the people feared the Lord,*
> *and believed the Lord and His servant Moses.*

Prior to this, God was known only as their Saviour and their Protector. After they went through the Red Sea, they feared and believed God as Lord. When we know God as Saviour, we expect Him to keep saving us from all our situations. When we know Him as protector, we expect God to deliver us. But when we know Him as Lord, we want to obey His Word and live by it. Our journey with God goes to a new level. That's what happens to us in the waters of baptism.

First, let's go back and look at dedication to the Lord. The only example we have in the Bible of a person being dedicated to God and then baptised in water later is Jesus. That's right—Jesus! Water baptism only existed for a little while before Jesus and it started with John the Baptist, but we'll consider that shortly.

We'll take a look at the life of Jesus and see what happened. He was dedicated (or presented) to the Lord in Luke 2:22–24:

> *Now when the days of her purification*
> *according to the law of Moses were completed,*
> *they brought Him to Jerusalem to present Him*
> *to the Lord (as it is written in the law of the*
> *Lord, every male who opens the womb shall be*
> *called holy to the Lord), and to offer a sacrifice*
> *according to what is said in the law of the Lord,*
> *a pair of turtledoves or two young pigeons.*

Joseph and Mary obeyed the Jewish law that God had given to Moses by dedicating (presenting) Jesus to the Lord. This is found in Leviticus12:2–8. Joseph and Mary were supposed to bring a lamb of the first year and a young pigeon or turtledove and if they couldn't bring a lamb, they could bring two turtledoves or two young pigeons. The Bible doesn't state why they chose the second offering but could it have been the fact that Mary was holding the Lamb of God (John1:29)? Maybe!

This event is significant, as Jesus, throughout his lifetime, maintained the law of God. His parents taught Him and He followed, starting with this event.

In church today, we don't bring sacrifices, but we dedicate (or present) babies to the Lord just like Jesus was dedicated to the Lord. The baby is prayed over by the pastors of the church and the parents are asked to bring the child up according to God's ways. This is the parents' decision. But there will come a time when God wants each person to decide to follow Him and water baptism is the public display.

Jesus was baptised in water as well, when he was older. This was a deliberate decision on His part to be baptised. He wasn't coerced into doing it but came willingly to His natural cousin, John. All four gospels give an account of Jesus' water baptism but we will look at the account in Matthew 3:13–17.

> *Then Jesus came from Galilee to John at the Jordan to be baptized by him. And John tried to prevent Him, saying, "I need to be baptized by You, and are You coming to me?" But Jesus answered and said to him, "Permit it to be so now, for thus it is fitting for us to fulfill all righteousness." Then he allowed Him. When He had been baptized, Jesus came up immediately from the water; and behold, the heavens were opened to Him, and He saw the Spirit of God descending like a dove and alighting upon Him. And suddenly a voice came from heaven, saying, "This is My beloved Son, in whom I am well pleased."*

This account is more detailed than all the others and we learn much more from it. As stated previously, Jesus came willingly to be baptised by John. John tried to prevent Him.

Why? John knew he was the one who came before Jesus to make the way. As such, he didn't feel worthy to baptise Jesus. However, there was a 'law' in place. John came from the tribe of Levi. We know this from Luke 1:5. John's father was a priest. Therefore, under the Old Covenant, John had the right to perform religious duties but Jesus didn't, as He came from the tribe of Judah. Therefore, John had to baptise Jesus. That is the reason Jesus told him to do it.

A further reason is that John was called to prepare the way for Jesus and until John had baptised Him, the way could not be open for Jesus to begin His ministry (Mark 1:2).

Another interesting point to note is that John was the first one to proclaim the message of repentance for the remission of sins through baptism (Luke 3:3). Jesus had never sinned so why did He need to be baptised? To fulfil what He requires us to do.

The verses also tell us that Jesus came up immediately from the water. It wasn't until the act of baptism was complete, that God spoke out and prophesied over His Son.

Once Jesus came up out of the water, the heavens opened and the Holy Spirit descended on Him. In our own lives, when we are water baptised, the Holy Spirit comes upon us and gives us more power over sin in our lives.

This is also the first time that God called Jesus His Son after Jesus was born. This is great for us, as it cements us as sons and daughters of God after we are baptised (Galatians 3:26-27). We don't just think it, but we come to know it.

Jesus was also baptised by John before He even started His ministry or was able to start His ministry. God isn't looking at what we do for Him, He's looking at the way we are obedient to Him in the things we do in life.

What about us? This episode in Jesus' life was written in the

Bible, not as a nice story but for us to follow. If Jesus was water baptised, then so should we be.

In Mark 16:16, the Bible tells us that:

> *He who believes and is baptized will be saved;*
> *but he who does not believe will be condemned.*

There is a believing and a baptism that are separate from being saved. The believing part is 'salvation'—when we're saved or transferred from the Kingdom of darkness to the Kingdom of light. This is sometimes done publicly or by inward confession.

The outward confession of that belief is water baptism. It shows the rest of the church (and the devil) that we were serious when we gave our lives to Jesus.

Peter's first sermon in Acts also highlights to the crowd (and us) that we need to both repent and be baptised and then receive the gift of the Holy Spirit.

Baptism is not just dunking in water. It's a symbolic act. Romans 6:2b–7 tells us the reason for this:

> *How shall we who died to sin live any longer in it? Or do you not know that as many of us as were baptized into Christ Jesus were baptized into His death? Therefore we were buried with Him through baptism into death, that just as Christ was raised from the dead by the glory of the Father, even so we also should walk in newness of life. For if we have been united together in the likeness of His death, certainly we also shall be in the likeness of His resurrection, knowing this, that our old man was*

> *crucified with Him, that the body of sin might be*
> *done away with, that we should no longer be slaves*
> *of sin. For he who has died has been freed from sin.*

Sin, in these verses, isn't referring to a specific act of sin, as we know we'll keep sinning (doing or thinking wrong things) until we go to heaven. These verses are talking about our sin nature—the natural side of us that, before we were saved, wanted to sin and keep on sinning because we didn't know any better until we had a revelation of who God is and what Jesus did for us on the cross and in the resurrection.

When we're baptised and are immersed in water, it's a symbol that as we go under, we (spiritually speaking) died with Jesus and as we come out of the water, we rise like Jesus did, walking in a new way of life. The sin nature has been broken off us. We no longer live in bondage as slaves to sin. We are free to live as God intended us to live—having a life and life more abundantly with every blessing that Jesus died to give us.

2 Peter 1:4 describes this so well:

> *by which have been given to us exceedingly great*
> *and precious promises, that through these you*
> *may be partakers of the divine nature, having*
> *escaped the corruption that is in the world*
> *through lust.*

We are now partakers of Christ's divine nature and new creatures in Christ Jesus. His divine nature is summed up as one word—love. Loving God and loving others is now our nature— our natural way of doing things. However, it's not as easy as that. We must renew our minds to the Word of God—reading, believing and confessing all the promises of God.

The Israelites had to walk through the water to leave Egypt far behind. They could have said no and been forced to fight the enemy themselves, but they would have been defeated. God wants us to choose in relation to baptism. There's still an enemy behind us, waiting to defeat us or there is the Promised Land in front of us, begging to be known and explored.

Water baptism is a choice and is usually a decision we make shortly after we give our lives to Jesus by talking with our spiritual leaders, for example, our pastors. If we don't choose to be water baptised, we'll still go to heaven if we have given our lives to Jesus (Romans 10:9-10). However, our journey will end at the Red Sea and we'll always have to contend with the sin nature. If we want to go forwards into the Promised Land and receive all God has for us here on earth, it will be necessary to make those steps.

There is another baptism, which is the baptism of the Holy Spirit. It will be covered later in this book. Generally speaking, water baptism comes prior to baptism in the Holy Spirit. but there are instances in the Book of Acts where it occurred in the reverse.

Just after the Israelites went through the Red Sea, they praised God for defeating their enemies. The song they sang is found in Exodus 15. There are a few elements to this song that are important for us to remember too. The first one is that it's the Lord who triumphs over our enemies. This can be by us taking our stand (whether that is being still or moving) and being obedient. There is a story in 2 Chronicles 20 where the enemies of Israel were coming against them. They didn't know what to do so they prayed to the Lord. The Spirit of the Lord came upon one of the men from the tribe of Levi who spoke these words out to the people (in part):

> *"You will not need to fight in this battle.*
> *Position yourselves, stand still and see the*
> *salvation of the Lord, who is with you."*

The Israelites didn't fight against the enemy, God did. All they had to do was position themselves to cross the Red Sea, get to the other side, stand still and see what God was about to do for them. This is the same for us. We can't fight the battle, only God can. We just need to run to Him, get His orders and stand still (or move, if that's what God requires) to see what God will do.

The second thing we need to remember is that the enemy fights against God. We may be the target but it's really God that the enemy is after. If the enemy can defeat us, he thinks he has defeated God, but that's not possible. He can only defeat us if we allow him to. It's not flesh and blood that comes against us but spiritual powers. We need to remember that when hard situations come against us.

The third thing is that God has mercy on us now that we're saved. He guides us through things and knows when we're weak. It's in our weaknesses that God is our strength. He bestows His mercy and His grace (undeserved favour) upon us. We shouldn't take the credit for our 'wins'. God needs to get and deserves all the glory.

The fourth thing is that winning this battle let the Israelites know that God would be with them in future battles. This is the hardest thing for us to remember as when we're in the midst of the next battle, it's difficult to remind ourselves that God has led us through before. He is always with us.

The fifth thing we need to remember is that God's promises will always come true and we need to have faith and trust that they will. The Israelites sang that God would plant them in the mountain of His inheritance. They believed He would bring them to the Promised Land and that all would be well.

The one thing to remember about the song the Israelites sang is that they were just starting on their journey, just like we do when we are saved and water baptised. The promises are out in front but we're now on the edge of the wilderness. This is the place where God needs to bring us to change our mindsets as we learn to trust Him, follow Him and love Him more.

We are at the edge of the wilderness ready to learn all that God has for us. It's going to be hard. But it will be worth it. You're now in training. Let's pray before we go further on our journey:

> *Father, we thank you that You're revealing to us Your purpose and Your plan for our lives. We thank you that you lead us in our journey step by step and not in a rush so we don't miss anything. Father, help us as we continue to be aware of when we sin so we can quickly repent and be restored onto the path again with you. In Jesus' name, amen.*

Chapter 4—The Wilderness: Provision

There is a saying that humans need three things for existence—shelter, food and love. Now we'll look at how God provides for us as we follow the Israelites' story.

The essential things for provision are water, food, clothing and shelter. Shelter was already taken care of as previously we discussed the cloud covering them by day and fire by night. The Bible also advises us that they had tents. So their needs in this area were met.

The clothing part was also met as the Bible tells us in Deuteronomy 8:4 that their clothing didn't wear out nor did their feet swell during the time they spent in the wilderness. Imagine wearing the same clothes for 40 years. I can't but for the Israelites, this was another part of the miraculous provision of God.

For us, both shelter and clothing are received the same way as food so they'll also be covered in this part of the chapter.

Water

Let's pretend we're in the Israelites' shoes as they came out of Egypt. We've packed all our belongings and the Egyptians have given us extra. However, we don't know how long this journey will take. We can only carry so much water and food. We have cattle and other animals that we could eat, but if we did, what would we use for sacrifices? We would come to the Promised Land with nothing.

As we were going out of Egypt, we knew in our hearts that God would provide. It seemed so easy to believe back then when we were so excited about the journey. But three days after we crossed the Red Sea, there's an issue. We haven't got enough water to drink so we need to find some for us and our animals. But where?

Just ahead some of us give a shout—they've found water at Marah (Exodus 15:22–27). However, those waters are as the name Marah suggests—they are bitter. Now what? Time to start complaining!

We know from our story so far that when we're saved, God provides everything we need. When Jesus died on the cross, He said, 'It is finished.' Everything God intended for us to have is given back to us if we believe in Jesus. But we know from our own story that God doesn't hand us things on a silver platter. We have to go back and remember the way we were saved—by believing and confessing. If we complain to God, He won't hear us. God only hears faith cries.

Back to the story of the Israelites -they started to complain against Moses. Moses cried out to God. God showed Moses a tree and He cast it into the waters and the waters were made sweet. But this was not a handout, but a prelude to a test from God. God showed them that He could provide their 'water' needs in the wilderness but there was a lesson to be learned and a new name of God to be remembered.

Verse 26 tells us:

> *"'If you diligently heed the voice of the Lord your God and do what is right in His sight, give ear to His commandments and keep all His statutes, I will put none of the diseases on you which I have brought on the Egyptians. For I am the Lord who heals you."*

But wait, you say, God only provided them with water and now He promises them His healing if they'll listen and obey His commandments. How does that work, especially for us? God was showing us that the way He'd healed the waters from bitter to sweet, He will turn our diseases and sicknesses into divine healing if we will trust and obey His commandments.

This is further confirmed in the New Testament. In Ephesians 5:26, it states:

> *that He [Jesus] might sanctify and cleanse her with the washing of water by the word.*

If we keep the Word of God and allow it to wash over us, cleanse us and refresh us each day, we'll find that we're set apart and will walk in divine health. This is a covenant between us and God. He turns the bitter things in our lives into sweet things as we obey Him and allow the work that Jesus did on the cross for us to become real in our lives.

I like what verse 27 tells us. It states that when they came to Elim, which was the next place, there were 12 wells of water and 70 palm trees. God tested the Israelites and then provided an abundant supply. God does that in our lives too. He tests us (not by sin or temptation) but with our obedience to His Word. If we need something, ask, hear what God says, and obey. The time between those three things may be quick or it may be long, but whatever time it takes, God will always provide for our needs if we are faithful to His Word.

Food and Clothing

Exodus 16 instructs us on how God provided food for the children of Israel. In verse 2, instead of asking, they again complained against Moses and Aaron (like they could feed them all). This is what we do sometimes. We complain against our pastors and leaders, thinking they should meet all our needs, when God is waiting for us to have faith in Him. God is the only one that can meet all our needs—not your job, your family, your pastor, the government—only God.

In verse 3, the Israelites reminisced, for they said, 'In Egypt we had pots of meat and we ate bread to the full.' Hang on a minute, weren't they slaves in Egypt? They may have had full bellies (which I doubt) but they didn't have full and free lives, which God wanted to give them.

God didn't address their complaints. Instead, He told Moses what He would do to fix the situation. God never addresses our complaints, He only provides the answers. That is what faith is—the ability to see the answer spiritually before we can see it in the physical (natural).

This time, their trust in God led them to having to do something. When the Israelites asked for water, Moses put the tree in and the waters became sweet. The Israelites did nothing for their cries (prayers) to be answered. This time, God led them on to the next step—that answers come only when we believe and step out. In this way, He was testing them (verse 4) to see whether they would be obedient to His Word.

The stepping out for the people meant that they would go out daily (in the morning) and gather a certain amount of manna each day but on the sixth day, they needed to go out and collect twice as much, as the seventh day was a day of rest. It's interesting to note that God provided for their provision of rest long before the Ten Commandments were given.

For us, there's both a spiritual hunger and a natural hunger for food. If we get the spiritual right, the natural will follow.

In our finite minds, we always worry about the natural things first, but God makes it clear in the Bible that we need to think differently about these things.

Matthew 6:25–34 teaches us about why we shouldn't worry and talks about natural happenings that we can see. Verse 33 is our key verse in this passage. It says:

> *But seek first the kingdom of God and His righteousness, and all these things shall be added to you.*

This verse tells us that, as Christians, we need to concentrate on the spiritual and the natural will take care of itself. In other words, if we do two things that run concurrently in our lives, natural things will come. Those two things are first to hunger for the principles of God and then to obey the laws and principles that God has set out.

Before we look at God's law regarding provision, let's look at what Jesus taught us about hungering for the Word of God. John chapter 6 is the main chapter to look at and refers to the manna that God gave the Israelites in Egypt. I will summarise the first part of the chapter and then we will look at the middle bit in-depth.

The first 14 verses of John chapter 6 tell the story of Jesus feeding the 5000 with five barley loaves and two small fish (not big ones like a shark). Jesus knew that to teach His disciples spiritual things, a natural event needed to take place for them to refer back to what He was teaching them. In this event, Jesus did the opposite of what He instructs us to do. First, He fed the multitudes using a small amount by turning the provision into a miracle. The disciples then gathered what was left.

In the next section of the chapter, Jesus walked on the water allowing the disciples' to experience a faith walk.

The next part of the chapter is what I want us to focus on. The very next day after Jesus and his disciples had crossed the lake, the crowd came looking for him. People will always come looking when there's natural provision. But this day, Jesus had a higher provision that He wanted them to know about. Verses 26 and 27 of chapter 6 point this out:

> *Jesus answered them and said, "Most assuredly, I say to you, you seek Me, not because you saw the signs, but because you ate of the loaves and were filled. Do not labour for the food which perishes, but for the food which endures to everlasting life, which the Son of Man will give you, because God the Father has set His seal on Him."*

Jesus didn't want them to be concerned with natural things. He wanted them to be more aware of the things that will fulfil their lives in a greater way. Jesus wants us to labour for the food that endures to everlasting life—to be about the Father's business (whatever that looks like for you). We need to follow the will of God for our lives and immerse ourselves in those pursuits. Is it always easy? No, it isn't, but it's always worth it.

Most of us, if we are honest with ourselves, have those times in our lives where we feel unfulfilled or just plain lonely and boring. If we seek the Kingdom of God and His righteousness, then we will step toward the things that God has for us. Once we do that, the natural things of provision will start flowing. If we're walking in God's will for our life, then we should be obeying God's Word.

Jesus goes on to say:

> *"I am the bread of life. He who comes to Me shall never hunger, and he who believes in Me shall never thirst"* and then *"I am the living bread which came down from heaven. If anyone eats of this bread, he will live forever, and the bread that I shall give is My flesh, which I shall give for the life of the world."*

Jesus died on the cross for us so that all provision could be ours, so we could live life and life more abundantly. We can't live an abundant life if all our needs aren't being met. But first, we have to obey the Word and live by it. Jesus is the Word of God made flesh, as John 1:14 tells us. That's why Jesus says to eat of His flesh. It doesn't mean literally eating His flesh, but it means reading the Word of God and studying it, then obeying it. The Word of God put into action has power in our lives to satisfy our hunger and eliminate those things that are not in God's will.

Just like we need to eat three to five meals a day to satisfy our natural hunger, we need to read the Word of God daily and obey it to satisfy our spiritual hunger. Just like the Israelites went out each morning to collect the manna and only collected enough for that day, except on the day before the Sabbath, we need to satisfy our spiritual hunger and collect the Word of God daily. Most people find mornings the best, before the busyness of the day sets in. If this doesn't work for you, find a suitable time through the day where you can read the Bible and get revelation from it. As you read, you'll find that the things you struggle with will become less of a struggle as the Word gets down into your heart and changes your life for the better.

The next step is to obey the laws and principles in God's Word. So what are they and is there a major principle that all God's Word runs on? The answer is yes—the major principle is the fact that everything we receive in the Kingdom of God is based on seed, time and harvest.

This principle is laid out in Genesis 8:22 which states:

> *"While the earth remains,*
> *Seedtime and harvest,*
> *Cold and heat,*
> *Winter and summer,*
> *And day and night*
> *Shall not cease."*

This is the major principle in God's Word. When we seek God's kingdom and His righteousness (His way of doing things) then it always begins with this principle. So let's look at the three things individually but to adjust our thinking just a bit, let's look at the farmer.

We'll pretend we're grain growers and planting wheat. The first thing we need to do is prepare the soil so that we have good planting conditions. The next thing is to buy some good seed to plant. We only have seeds but we expect that, in planting them, we are going to reap a harvest. We can't see it in the natural, but our imagination takes over and we can see it there. After we have planted, we need to water and fertilise it and make sure we pull out any weeds. We don't want our plants getting choked or dying due to lack of water or food.

The most enduring step in this process is waiting for those plants to produce wheat. First, we look for the little stems that come out of the ground, then we look for the leaves and then we wait for the plant to grow. Then, we harvest our wheat. All of this can take weeks to years. Some of the wheat we grind up and bake into bread to eat and some we send to market. We know that our wheat is really good, so we keep some seeds from them to plant next time.

This is the same process we use with our spiritual seed. Our seed starts off as natural, becomes supernatural in time and then natural again at the harvest. This is difficult for us to understand as we live in a physical world, one where we can touch, taste, see, smell and hear. But God has a different system and that's why we need to seek His way of doing things. God always operates with a natural seed but in the supernatural realm. So what are our seeds?

The first one is our money and this requires our complete trust in God for our provision. What value does money have to you? Generally, it's the amount paid to you for your time and talent. Some people also receive money because of the generosity of others or from the government. Money generally buys our food or the seed to grow the food. Sometimes, we use our possessions to pay for our food. So, if money is important to us, how does God want us to use it to show our trust in Him?

Verse 24 of Matthew 6 tells us that we cannot serve two masters. The reason for that is that we can only love one of them, which means we hate the other. As humans, we need to choose God or mammon (for example, money) to serve. If we serve mammon, it means we hate God or we don't trust His ways of doing things—we despise it. If we trust in God, then we will do things God's way and fully trust in Him.

So how do we trust God with our money? We need to go back

to the Old Testament. You may ask why. After all, we're living in the times of the New Testament between Acts and Revelation. The reason that this principle is not mentioned in the New Testament is that for the people writing the New Testament, it was a principle, a way of life for them. The principle I'm talking about is tithing.

Malachi 3:8 states the following:

> *"Will a man [or woman] rob God? Yet you have robbed Me! But you say, in what way have we robbed You? In tithes and offerings."*

Verse 10 of the same chapter gives the people the directions on what to do and why. It states:

> *"Bring all the tithes into the storehouse, that there may be food in My house, and try Me now in this," says the Lord of hosts, "if I will not open for you the windows of heaven and pour out for you such blessing that there will not be room enough to receive it."*

Robbing God sounds like a bad thing for us to do, but in robbing God, we are robbing ourselves of the blessings He wants to pour out on us.

I can tell you from experience that if you give God your tithe (10% of your gross income) then God will turn the 90% into 100%. How does He do it? I have yet to find out, but in my life when I have needed things, the money has been there to pay for them.

I spent three years as a single mother. My children and I never went without and most of the time I couldn't tell you why. I remember one instance where I had over $1000 worth of bills due in one month and not enough income to pay for them and all the necessities of the family. By the end of the month, I had not only paid the $1000 but we never went without the basics. From what I remember, nobody gave us any extra. It was all God.

The verse in Malachi says if we tithe, then blessing will come to our house. Blessing in the Bible means a wish or prayer for favourable circumstances. For us, favourable circumstances mean all our needs are met. For example, enough clothing, food, a good job and a loving family.

Blessings will mean different things to different people. For example, if you are starving, a blessing of food is appropriate, or if your car just doesn't work, a blessing may mean a new car. Blessings are individual and not corporate. God meets our needs individually because that's how much He loves us.

The next seed we can sow is our time and talents (or our gifts). These will be looked at later in the book as we continue to follow the story of the Israelites.

Before we continue our journey, let's pray:

> *Father, we thank you for Your Word that You have given to us. Please open our eyes as we read it so we can know how to live our lives better following your principles. Let the Word of God wash over us and cleanse us and allow the Word to satisfy our spiritual hunger. Help us to find a time in our daily lives to devote to You. In Jesus' name, amen.*

Chapter 5— The Wilderness: Worship and Unity

Let's continue our journey with the Israelites. So far, we've given our lives to Jesus and allowed Him to be our Saviour and Lord. We've been baptised in water and discovered how God provides us with our provisions through obedience to His Word.

In this chapter, we're going to cover the power of worship and the power of unity and using the gifts God has given us. These elements are necessary if we are to grow individually in the church environment. A further chapter in this book will be dedicated to what 'church' looks like for us.

First, let's discover what worship is and how powerful it is in defeating the enemy.

In the dictionary, one meaning of worship is homage or service paid to God, adoration felt or shown for a person or principle. The second part is what I love—worship is the adoration I feel and show to God. In the dictionary, 'adoration' means regard with deep respect and affection. This is the spot that God wants in our lives—the number one spot. For what reason? He's our creator, redeemer and knows us intimately inside and out. What other reason do we need? We were created to worship God and follow His good path for our lives.

For the Israelites, this was the main reason for leaving Egypt. It was never about the Promised Land to start with but about setting aside time to worship God. Exodus chapter 5:1–3 gives us the story of Moses' first encounter with Pharaoh before the Israelites left Egypt. It states, in part:

> *"Let My people go, so that they may hold a feast to Me in the wilderness ... Please let us go three days' journey into the desert and sacrifice to the Lord our God, lest He fall upon us with pestilence or with the sword."*

This was the reason the Israelites left Egypt—to go and sacrifice to God (or worship God). In the footnotes of my Bible, it states that feasts were community activities when the community would stop its normal activity to offer thanksgiving to certain deities on specific occasions. It was usually a joyous time of eating and worship. It was a time set apart to worship God—to adore Him and thank Him for all He had done for them.

The Israelites haven't come to that place in our journey yet. But on the way there, a battle occurred that shows us the power of worship in obtaining victory. Exodus 17:8–16, tells the story of victory over the Amalekites. Moses commanded Joshua to go out in the valley and fight the Amalekites. Whilst he was doing that, Moses, Aaron and Hur went to the top of the hill. However, they weren't going to have a picnic and rest while the others fought the battle. No, they were going to fight too, just in a different way.

That different way involved Moses holding up his hands. What? That doesn't sound like the way to win the battle. Now, if he was firing crossbows that might be different, but just raising his hands doesn't sound like it would do much. Read a little further on in the story. In verse 11, it states:

> *And so it was, when Moses held up his hand, that Israel prevailed; and when he let down his hand, Amalek prevailed.*

This is a powerful natural illustration of what happens when we stand and lift our hands toward God. As long as we are worshipping God, the enemy will not prevail against us. It doesn't matter how fierce the battle is, if we just worship God (adore Him and thank Him for everything He has done for us and is going to do), then it throws the enemy into confusion and they leave because they can't handle it; it doesn't make sense to them. It probably doesn't make much sense to us either, but if we're obedient to God, it doesn't matter if it doesn't make sense, we should just do it.

When Moses' hands became heavy, he sat down, but still, the Israelites kept winning because his hands were still up. Sometimes, the battle we face can become heavy, but it doesn't matter if we change our posture, as long as we keep worshipping.

After a while, Moses' hands couldn't stay up any longer because the battle seemed never-ending. However, it wasn't time to quit; it was time to enlist assistance. This came from Aaron and Hur, who held Moses' hands up until the sun went down. That's a long time to hold your hands up.

When the battle gets too strong, we need to enlist the assistance of others, not those who'll gossip and tell everyone what our battle is, but those we know we can trust to hold up our hands—to encourage us to keep going because God has got it and is with us.

For the Israelites, the battle was won with worship. The ones on the ground had no idea why they were sometimes winning and sometimes losing, but Moses, Aaron and Hur did. We need to be sensitive to the leading of the Holy Spirit and find out His battle plan for us. Galatians 6:9 states:

*And let us not grow weary while doing good,
for in due season we shall reap; if we do not lose
heart.*

When the battle gets strong and long, keep going, you're nearly there. Don't get tired of doing what God says or give up because it appears it's not working. Like the Israelites, the battle will be won if we don't give up or lose heart or even lose our trust in God and the power of His Word.

Continue to worship God, even when things aren't going great. If you persist, the enemy will give up. James 4:7 encourages us to go on. It states:

*Therefore, submit to God. Resist the devil and
he will flee from you.*

Moses submitted to God by holding his hands up in his own strength and then with assistance. When he did this, the enemy was eventually defeated and destroyed. In the same way, we need to submit first to God by being obedient to Him and the Word. It's only then that we have the power (through God and His Word) to resist the devil. He will then flee because he has no power against the Word of God.

Worship is not just a slow song that we sing on Sundays but a lifestyle of being obedient to God and His Word. Incorporate this into your daily life and you'll see the enemy flee away. He might be silly enough to come back and attack you in some other way, but if you use the Word of God, he'll always have to flee.

The next concept we're going to look at in this chapter is unity and using the gifts God has given us. Why do I put these together? I believe that a church can't be in unity unless all the people in the church are using their gifts. When we're in unity, there's no jealousy, backstabbing or gossip, as we all work together in the place that God has designed specifically for us.

First, we're going to look at the Israelites. This story only relates to a portion of them receiving their gifts, but it will give us an insight into how it works with unity.

In the dictionary, unity means, in part, being formed of parts that constitute a whole due to the coherence of parts. Even though we're all individuals, the body of Christ must walk together as one body, each part having its own unique function. This is much like our natural body. We are one but we are made up of individual parts. We'll discuss this more later in relation to the church today.

The story of the Israelites related to this is found in Exodus 18. It's the story of Jethro's advice to Moses. Jethro was Moses' father-in-law as well as being the priest of Midian so he had lots of wisdom to give.

Jethro came into the camp and heard how God had delivered the Israelites from Egypt. He stayed with them for a while and observed what was going on in the camp.

In verse 13, Moses was the judge of all the Israelites and the people stood before him with their issues from morning to night. Just think about it. You go to work in the daytime and your job is to be a judge and counsellor to over one million people. Now granted, not all of them would have come on the same day. But even so, if one thousand of them came, Moses would judge and counsel on their issues from morning to evening. It would be enough to wear anyone out.

Jethro saw this happening and told Moses it wasn't good as both he and the people would wear themselves out (verse 18).

Sometimes, we try and do too much, either in the church, at home or at work or sometimes in all three places. We wonder why we're stressed and God doesn't heal us. It's because we are violating His laws of rest and the power of unity.

Jethro gave Moses counsel on this issue. He told him to stand before God and select from the people certain able men with qualifications of character who would be able to stand with him and judge and counsel the people. However, not all the men were to be given equal tasks. Some would judge thousands, some hundreds, some fifties and some tens (verse 21) God set up a hierarchal structure according to each one's abilities to meet the needs of all the Israelites.

Those men were instructed to judge the small matters, but still give Moses the bigger ones. I love what verse 22b states, which is:

> *So it will be easier for you, for they will bear the burden with you.*

Those men and Moses would be in unity—they would bear the burden together. Although they had different roles, each one would do their part and it would be easier for Moses but also easier for them. They would feel fulfilled and grow in their leadership skills as they would be using their gifts.

It's interesting to note that after this, Jethro left. He was called to the camp for two reasons. The first reason was to unite Moses with his wife and sons (they had been staying with Jethro) and the other reason was to provide wisdom and counsel. Jethro wasn't called to lead a million or so Israelites, but he was called to give counsel to their leader when desperately needed. In that, they both fulfilled the purpose of God equally.

What about us? How does this story apply to our lives? Simple—we are each called uniquely by God to fulfil the purpose He's planned for us. However, we can only do that when we're connected to God and connected to His Church. In 1 Corinthians 12:12, 18, 25–27, the Bible is clear regarding this issue for us:

> *For as the body is one and has many members, but all the members of that one body, being many, are one body, so also is Christ.*

> *But now God has set the members, each one of them, in the body just as He pleased.*

> *… that there should be no schism (division) in the body, but that the members should have the same care for one another. And if one member suffers, all the members suffer with it; or if one member is honoured, all the members rejoice with it. Now you are the body of Christ, and members individually.*

We can see from these verses that even though we're all individuals, God has placed us in His body together with others. Not so we can compete, but so we can use our gifts and talents to perform our part of the body's function. For example, in our own body, the heart has a different function from the eye but I have never heard them in competition for the other one's part.

Psalm 133:1 tells us that 'Behold, how good and how pleasant it is for brethren to dwell together in unity!' Unity in this verse is the Hebrew word *yachad*, which means 'alike', 'together' and 'only'. It doesn't mean we have to agree with each other all the time but that our main goal in the church is to work towards one common goal—to see our nation and the world come to know Jesus as their Saviour and their Lord.

In Ephesians 4:13–16, it advises us on how we grow in maturity in God. First, we need to come to the unity of the faith—believing in Jesus and his life, death, burial and resurrection. Then we need to have knowledge of Jesus—of the way He operated on earth and the way we should operate in our lives. From that, we become a perfect man (or woman). Our perfection won't happen whilst we're here on earth, but that should be our goal. How does this happen? By speaking the truth in love and growing in all the things that Jesus wants for us.

Verses 15b and 16 then tell us the result of all of us, in unity, doing this same thing in our own lives:

> *Who is the head—Christ—from whom the whole body, joined and knit together by what every joint supplies, according to the effective working by which every part does its share, causes growth of the body the edifying of itself in love.*

The result is that the body of Christ will be joined and knit together by what each person in the body supplies by doing their part. It causes growth in the whole body, including you and me. What growth does God want to see in us the most? It is the growth of our love walk. If we love God and love others, then the body of Christ will grow. How does this happen? It happens through unity and togetherness.

Jesus prayed this in John 17:20–26. This was one of the final prayers Jesus prayed prior to dying on the cross and being raised again. In case you're wondering, His last prayer was 'Father, forgive them for they know not what they do.' Therefore, if this was one of the last prayers recorded, it must have some insight into the outcomes Jesus expected from all of his disciples, including us.

Four times in those verses Jesus prays that 'they also may be one'. Jesus knew that unity was powerful but there are three stages to unity. These verses show us the progression. In verse 20, Jesus tells us who He's praying for. This is the first stage. We must believe and confess before unity can be granted.

> *I do not pray for these alone, but also for those*
> *who will believe in Me through their word.*

This verse instructs us that this prayer not only applied to his current 11 disciples (by then Judas had betrayed Him) but to all those who believe in Jesus through confession. That includes you and me. Note that again the principle of believing and confessing is evident.

Verse 21 tells us about the second stage of unity:

> *That they all may be one, as You, Father, are in*
> *Me, and I in You; that they also may be one in*
> *Us, that the world may believe that You sent Me.*

This stage is really the next two stages melded together. We need to be in unity together and then we'll be in unity with

Jesus and God. God and Jesus are in such unity that they think alike, act alike and speak alike. That's what we as the body of believers are supposed to be like. When Satan looks at us, he can't tell us apart because we all think alike, act alike and speak alike because we have been recreated in the image of Jesus.

The reason for us being in unity is not to have a love-in session, but that those in the world may believe that Jesus was sent by God to redeem them as well. We're already in the family, but others need to join. We must do our utmost to stay in unity.

As I said before, we don't need to agree on everything but we must all agree with God's main principles in His Word. They are set out for us in Ephesians 4:4–6. From verses 1 to 6 it's called 'walk in unity'. This is what we are to believe:

> *There is one body and one Spirit, just as you*
> *were called in one hope of your calling: one*
> *Lord, one faith, one baptism, one God and*
> *Father of all, who is above all, and through all,*
> *and in you all.*

If we can agree with this, we will 'walk worthy of the calling with which you were called, with all lowliness and gentleness, with longsuffering, bearing with one another in love, endeavouring to keep the unity of the Spirit in the bond of peace.' (verses 1–3)

This is what unity looks like. When the church of Jesus Christ walks in unity, God commands a blessing (an empowerment to prosper in all that the church puts her mind to).

Let's pray before we move forward in our journey.

> *Father, we thank you that You have set out what unity means clearly in Your Word. As we continue to walk with You, show us where we need to change to have unity with all believers in You so that we may walk in your complete blessing. In Jesus' name, amen.*

Chapter 6—The Wilderness: Our Covenant

Covenant—that's a big word and one that's not used in the western world much anymore. We talk about contracts and entering into agreements but these can easily become invalid.

For example, if I enter into a contract to buy a house, I will usually make it conditional on either obtaining finance or getting a pest inspection or a building inspection to make sure there's no structural damage. If one of those conditions is not finalised, then I can easily terminate the contract and am no longer bound to buy that house. But what about covenant? How is that different from contracts or agreements between two people?

One of the meanings of covenant in the dictionary is 'bound' or 'secured by'. In other words, there's no getting out of it, except through death. As a result, covenant appears to be a scary word. It means if we make a covenant with someone, only death will get us out of it. We have to be really sure it's what we want to do.

When we make a covenant with someone, some thought has to go into it. Take a marriage covenant. Even though in the world we live in, a marriage covenant is not all that secure (it wasn't in Jesus' day either (Matthew 19: 7)), it is a good example and a covenant most of us are familiar with.   It's easy to get out of the marriage covenant in a physical sense, but emotionally, it may be quite difficult.

To form a marriage covenant, there must be two persons, generally a male and a female. There is a ceremony called a wedding to seal that covenant. At that ceremony, the male makes promises to the female and vice versa. They promise that they're going to be there for one another through thick and thin. Where one person is weak, the other will be strong and the other way around.

The other element of a covenant is shedding blood. In times past, in a wedding ceremony, they cut the skin on the left ring finger on each hand and mingled the blood. These days we swap wedding rings to signify the covenant (this is much better, I think).

It's basically forming a partnership with someone that can only be broken through the death of one of the parties (unless you live in our world). This is how God created it to be. Don't feel bad if you're divorced, as God will forgive you as He has forgiven me.

There are many covenants that God made with people in the Bible, starting with the first one in Genesis and ending with the last one, which is the one we discussed in a previous chapter—where Jesus died on the cross for you and me so that the covenant relationship between God and man could be restored. You and I have the opportunity to enter into this covenant if we so choose. If we don't, we face the consequences of eternity without God. Covenant is always by choice, never by force.

As we journey with the Israelites, we see that God made a covenant with them too. This is what is known as the Law in the Bible. We no longer live under that law because another covenant (as mentioned above) has been given. You can still choose to live under this covenant (like the Jews do) but the last one is so much better.

The Israelites have now come to the Wilderness of Sinai (Exodus 19:1). When Moses went to Pharaoh for the first time, he advised Pharaoh that God had told the Israelites to take a three-day journey into the wilderness to hold a feast for Him (Exodus 5:1). They had now reached that place, but they arrived there in the third month, not the third day. This is where God affirmed His covenant with the children of Israel. In verses 3b to 6 of Exodus chapter 19, God is speaking to Moses to tell the Israelites the following:

> *"Thus you shall say to the house of Jacob, and tell the children of Israel: You have seen what I did to the Egyptians, and how I bore you on eagles' wings and brought you to Myself. Now therefore, if you will indeed obey My voice and keep My covenant, then you shall be a special treasure to Me above all people; for all the earth is Mine. And you shall be to me a kingdom of priests and a holy nation. These are the words which you shall speak to the children of Israel."*

What covenant were the children of Israel to keep? The covenant that God was about to advise them of. Before they could enter into this covenant with God, a few things had to happen. They are:

1. The Israelites had to agree to the covenant after God had laid out the terms. If the Israelites hadn't agreed, there would have been no covenant. In verse 7, Moses called for the elders of the people and told them all that God had said. The people answered in verse 8, 'All that the Lord has spoken we will do'. God laid out His request to form a covenant with them and they responded with a 'Yes, we will do it.'

2. The second thing Moses had to do was consecrate the people for two days and then they all had to wash their clothes (verses 10–11 and 14–15). This means they all had to separate themselves from their normal pursuits and cleanse themselves so they could stand in the presence of God when He advised them of the covenant and ratified it with them. The people had two days to do this and on the third day, God was going to come and visit them.

3. The next thing was that the covenant had to be spoken. This covenant contained the requirements that God was going to keep and the requirements that the Israelites were going to keep. If each kept their side of the covenant, it would remain strong. But if one side didn't fulfil their requirements, then the covenant would be broken and would require a sacrifice.

In Exodus 20, the covenant was spoken, which was what we know as the Ten Commandments. These Ten Commandments contain two different sets of laws—one was the Israelites' relationship with God and its requirements and the second was the Israelites' relationship with each other and its requirements. There are six commandments relating to God and four commandments relating to each other.

After that, God proceeded to set out His judgements or the decisions of the Law. These included laws concerning servants, violence, animal control, responsibility for property, moral and ceremonial principles, justice for all, Sabbath and three annual feasts they were to keep. This is much like the laws of today that the government of all levels in our nations set. These laws make life easier and safer for all.

God also set out His part of the covenant for bringing them into the Promised Land and the way they should live once they arrived. An angel was going before them to keep them in the way and to bring them into the Promised Land. Some of the promises that God made to the Israelites are found in Exodus 23:21–33 and are:

Verse	God's promise	Israelites' requirement
21	I will pardon your transgressions	Beware of the angel, obey His voice and don't provoke Him
22	He will be an enemy to your enemies and an adversary to your adversaries	Obey the angel's voice and do all that God says
23	God will cut off all enemies	Follow the angel
24–25	Serve God and He will bless your food and water and take sickness away from the midst of you. No one will suffer miscarriage or be barren. God will fulfil the number of your days.	Don't bow down to the gods of the people whose land you are promised or serve them, nor do according to their works
32–33	The people will remain there and be a snare to you	Don't make a covenant with their gods nor let the people dwell in the land with you

In Exodus 24:1–9, Israel affirmed this whole covenant with God. Remember, for a covenant to be ratified, blood must be shed and there must be an agreement between the parties. In this case, God set out the agreement they were to follow and what His part in it was and what their part was. However, they couldn't just listen, they had to agree. This is another part of believing and confessing. In verse 3, the Israelites said:

> "All the words which the Lord has said we will do."

The Israelites had now agreed to the covenant and then blood had to be shed. In verse 4, Moses built an altar and 12 pillars to the Lord. The 12 pillars represented the 12 tribes of Israel and was their way of showing they were all in agreement. They then offered burnt offerings and peace offerings of oxen to the Lord. The blood was sprinkled on the altar and the people. The following words spoken by Moses, in verse 8, ratified the covenant:

> "This is the blood of the covenant which the Lord
> has made with you according to all these words."

The ceremony was now complete and the covenant came into effect from that day forth.

How does this apply to us? Are we under a covenant? Yes, we are. As soon as we gave our lives to Jesus, we agreed to the covenant. We believed that Jesus died on the cross for our sins (blood was shed) and we confessed that we believed in Jesus (our agreement). We can now join the family of God and receive all the blessings God has for us. Like the Israelites, those blessings are many. We have discussed this in an earlier chapter. It's commonly known as salvation.

The book of Hebrews sets out how our covenant came into being and the reason it's so much better than the one the Israelites were under. The new covenant which we live under is faultless. Hebrews 8:7 states:

> *For if that first covenant had been faultless, then no place would have been sought for a second.*

It then goes on to say in Hebrews that God said that because the Israelites didn't continue in the covenant, God disregarded them and had to make a new covenant that was faultless. To do that, God had to make a covenant where the sacrifice was perfect and the people's hearts could be changed so that the laws (or commandments) could be written on their hearts. God would then be merciful through that covenant and our sins would be remembered no more.

How did that new covenant come into being? God had to set up the covenant first. Usually, as we have seen with the Israelites, the first party sets out the terms of the agreement, the second party listens to those terms and then agrees, and finally, a blood sacrifice is made to confirm the covenant. The covenant God set up for us is the other way around. The blood sacrifice was made first by Jesus dying on the cross. Then the terms of the covenant were made by God, which states that:

- We must believe that Jesus died in our place (as our sacrifice)
- We must believe that His death was not a normal earthly death
- We must believe that God raised Jesus from the dead

If we do that, then the covenant of salvation is ours.
So now we are in covenant with God. What next? We must

be like the Israelites and keep the terms of the covenant. They are called the commandments in the Bible. For us, the Ten Commandments have been turned into two—love God and love others. If we do this, we'll always obey all God's commandments.

This is easier said than done. Have you ever gone through your day and loved everybody you have come across? I'm sure you haven't, just like me.

We only have two commandments but they cover our whole life—our relationship with God and our relationship with others. If we love God fully and completely, we'll love His creation—people. God didn't say they had to love us, just that we have to love them. Of course, if they're Christians and under the same covenant, the same commandments apply to them.

What if we fail (which we will)? That's what repentance is for—when we mess up.

With the Israelites, the high priest had to make a sacrifice of certain animals each year for the Israelites, so that sins they'd committed unknowingly would be forgiven. For the ones they knew about, it was a daily sacrifice at the altar. For them, 'forgiven' meant covered over and not washed clean. They were still living with the guilt, as their consciences weren't cleansed like ours are under the new covenant.

Under the new covenant, Jesus is only required to die once. This is affirmed to us in Hebrews 9:26b.

> [B]ut now, once at the end of the ages, He has appeared to put away sin by the sacrifice of Himself.

In verse 28a, the Bible goes on to state:

> [S]o Christ was offered once to bear the sins of many.

We'll consider the reasons for Jesus only dying once when we look at the role of the high priest. For the Israelites, the sacrifice had to be perfect. It tells us in the Bible that Jesus was our perfect sacrifice. He never sinned, so he was perfect. Under this covenant, our sins were forever cleansed and our guilt is only cleansed when we come to know Jesus and repent of our sins.

Let's thank God for the covenant that He made with and for us. God made this covenant with man before any of us had ever accepted it. God would have made it even if it was just you. Let's pray:

> *Father, we thank you that we are in covenant with you. We thank you that Jesus died on the cross for our sins and that we could be forgiven. We know that we're strong because You are strong and we have the same rights as Jesus because we are in covenant with You. We thank you that we are your sons and daughters. In Jesus' name, amen.*

Chapter 7—The Wilderness: Our Priesthood

For the covenant to be further ratified for the Israelites, a temple needed to be built. There needed to be a place to conduct sacrifices. This place had to be approved by God and be holy. It was only a holy sacrifice that was going to appease God when the Israelites didn't keep their side of the covenant.

In Exodus 24:12, God told Moses to meet with Him on the mountain so that He could write the laws and commandments on tablets of stone. Further, God told Moses to build a temple and furnishings. God gave Moses the pattern of the tabernacle and the pattern of the furnishings. Where did God get these patterns from? The earthly tabernacle and furnishings are exact copies of what is in heaven (Hebrews 9:23).

The tabernacle was comprised of two parts—the Holy Place and the Most Holy Place. The Holy Place was where the priests went to offer sacrifices. It contained a lampstand, a table and the showbread, and is commonly called the sanctuary (Hebrews 9:2). The Most Holy Place contained a golden censer and the Ark of the Covenant. The Ark of the Covenant contained a gold pot that had the manna, Aaron's rod that budded and the tablets on which God wrote the commandments (Hebrews 9:3–4). The mercy seat was on top of the Ark of the Covenant.

Moses came down from the mountain and they started to build the tabernacle. This was later called the temple when Solomon built the first temple to replace the tabernacle.

Do we have a temple? Most of us think it's the church building where we worship, but God is more specific than that. He wants to be able to commune with us and for us to commune with Him daily. So the temple is no longer made with wood and man-made materials. It is actually you and me—bodies that house the Holy Spirit. It tells us this in 1 Corinthians 3:16:

> *Do you not know that you are the temple of God and that the Spirit of God dwells in you?*

Further, in 1 Corinthians 6:19–20, it states:

> *Or do you not know that your body is the temple of the Holy Spirit who is in you, whom you have from God, and you are not your own? For you were bought at a price; therefore glorify God in your body and in your spirit, which are God's.*

Christians are now the temple of God. Does this mean we don't have to go to church anymore? No, but it does mean that you don't have to go to a place to sacrifice when you sin. You can repent and ask God to forgive you any time of the day and night, as He is indwelling in you.

Let's explore what the temple (church) is for us today. Hebrews 10:24–25 gives us a clear indication of what church is for us. It states:

> *And let us consider one another in order to stir up love and good works, not forsaking the assembling of ourselves together, as is the manner of some, but exhorting one another, and so much the more as you see the Day approaching.*

In Ephesians 4:11–13a, we read the purpose of apostles, prophets, evangelists, pastors and teachers (fivefold ministry). Those callings and gifts are given to some people for:

> *[T]he equipping of the saints for the work of the*
> *ministry, for the edifying of the body of Christ,*
> *till we all come to the unity of the faith and of the*
> *knowledge of the Son of God.*

We attend church, not because the building is the church (as we have seen, we are) but so we can be stirred up to love and do good works as we go out into our workplaces, schools, homes and wherever else we go during the week. It's a place of encouragement and also so that the fivefold ministry can equip us to go out and do what God has called us to do. This is the purpose of the church today and the reason why we are the temple of God. We don't have to wait for the pastors to do the work—they equip us to do the work.

What is that work? Mark 16:15–18 tells us what that work is. It's called the Great Commission and is what Jesus instructed His church to do after He returned to heaven. Jesus told us:

> *"Go into all the world and preach the gospel to*
> *every creature. He who believes and is baptized*
> *will be saved; but he who does not believe will be*
> *condemned. And these signs will follow those who*
> *believe: In My name they will cast out demons;*
> *they will speak with new tongues; they will take up*
> *serpents; and if they drink anything deadly, it will*
> *by no means hurt them; they will lay hands on the*
> *sick, and they will recover."*

This is the job that Jesus left for us to do as His temple. It won't look the same for everyone. Some will be in the marketplace showing Jesus to their colleagues, others will be called into the fivefold ministry, some will travel the world preaching about Jesus, some will go into schools, some will write on the internet so the world can read it and some will leave all to go to a foreign land.

Whatever Jesus has given you to do, is what you should do. Don't be jealous of another's calling, just find out what your unique calling is and you will be content knowing you're walking in God's will.

The final thing regarding the covenant is that there must be a high priest and priests to minister to the Lord in the tabernacle. Exodus 28:1 tells us who the priests were that God appointed when it states:

> *"Now take Aaron your brother, and his sons*
> *with him, from among the children of Israel,*
> *that he may minister to Me as priest."*

The priests might have been appointed by God but there were still conditions to fulfil. Exodus 28:41 sets out those conditions:

> *So you shall put them (the special clothes) on*
> *Aaron your brother and on his sons with him.*
> *You shall anoint them, consecrate them, and*
> *sanctify them, that they may minister to Me as*
> *priests.*

Then Exodus 28:2–40 tell us about the special clothes

Aaron and his sons were to wear whilst ministering as priests. When they weren't ministering, they could wear normal clothes but when they were ministering, they had to wear special clothes. These clothes were the only things that set them apart from the rest of the Israelites and represented the special position that God had given them.

Aaron had to wear more special garments when he went into the holy place. He was the only one allowed in there and he went once a year. Exodus 28:35 tells us:

> *And it [special robe] shall be upon Aaron when he ministers, and its sound will be heard when he goes into the holy place before the Lord and when he comes out, that he may not die.*

What sound? This robe was not only made of material but also had bells on it as a sign of worship to the Lord.

What about the high priest? Who was appointed to that role? The first mention of the high priest (for the Israelites) is in Leviticus 21:10 where it gives the requirements of the high priest:

> *"He who is the high priest among his brethren, on whose head the anointing oil was poured and who is consecrated to wear the garments, shall not uncover his head nor tear his clothes."*

The following verses go on to list a number of other requirements. Hebrews 5:4 confirms that Aaron was the high priest. Even though the book of Exodus doesn't specifically state that he was, it can be assumed as in Number 3:5-6, the Levites were to be brought before Aaron to serve him. This is further confirmed earlier in Exodus 29:1–8 where it tells us that Aaron was dressed in all the special garments—the tunic, the robe, the ephod and the breastplate, the woven band of the ephod, the turban and the holy crown. Aaron's sons only had tunics put on them.

Furthermore, the work in the temple was too much for Aaron and his sons, so who did God appoint? A tribe was chosen from among the Israelites—the tribe of Levi. This is shown in Numbers 3:6–9:

> *Bring the tribe of Levi near, and present them before Aaron the priest, that they may serve him ... And you shall give the Levites to Aaron and his sons; they are given entirely to him from among the children of Israel.*

Who is our high priest? Hebrews 4:14 states that Jesus is our high priest:

> *Seeing then that we have a great High Priest who has passed through the heavens, Jesus the Son of God, let us hold fast our confession.*

Jesus is our high priest, but he didn't come through the line of Levi but through the line of Judah, so how can this be?

To investigate this a little further, we have to go to the story just prior to John the Baptist's birth. His father Zachariah was a priest and in Luke 1:9 it tells us:

> *[A]ccording to the custom of the priesthood, his lot fell to burn incense when he went into the temple of the Lord.*

The only place in the tabernacle where you could burn incense was the altar of incense described in Exodus 30:1–10. It's interesting to note verses 7 and 8, which state:

> *Aaron shall burn on it sweet incense every morning; when he tends the lamps, he shall burn incense on it. And when Aaron lights the lamps at twilight, he shall burn incense on it, a perpetual incense before the Lord throughout your generations.*

It was Aaron who had to burn the incense—the high priest. So, when burning the incense, Zechariah was considered to be the high priest. An angel appeared to him and told him he was going to have a son in his old age and he would name him John.

Later on, we read in Luke 1:36 that Mary (Jesus' mother) was told that she was going to have a son and that Elizabeth, her relative, was also pregnant.

John the Baptist should have followed in his father's footsteps. He was the only son but was killed by King Herod.

At Jesus' trial, we hear of another high priest of that time called Caiaphas, who was high priest that year. Zachariah would have died long ago by this time. Jesus was questioned by the high priest in Mark 14:60–64 and Jesus' answers didn't sit well with him. The high priest then proceeded to tear his clothes (his priestly garments) in verse 63.

The law stated in Leviticus 21:10 under the regulations for the conduct of priests that:

> *He who is the high priest among his brethren, on whose head the anointing oil was poured and who is consecrated to wear the garments, shall not uncover his head **nor tear his clothes**. [emphasis added]*

Once this was done, that person could no longer be the high priest. So at Jesus' trial, there ceased to be a high priest who was consecrated.

A new covenant was just about to be introduced—one where Jesus was the sacrificial lamb and the covenant was between God and man (who believed in Jesus). A new high priest was needed for the new covenant to make intercession between God and man and that high priest was Jesus. No one else needs to be appointed, as Jesus lives forever (Hebrews 7:24).

What about the priests in the new covenant? Who are they? They are the ones that can now come boldly into the Holy of Holies (or the Holy Place). In Hebrews 4:16, it tells us this:

> *Let us therefore come boldly to the throne of grace, that we may obtain mercy and find grace to help in time of need.*

The throne of grace (where God's presence was) was over the mercy seat, which was on the Ark of the Covenant (Exodus 25:22). It was a place of sacrifice and a place of mercy for the Israelites once per year, but we can ask for forgiveness and obtain mercy anytime because we can come to that throne freely.

But who are these ones? Revelation 1:5b–6 describes them:

> *To Him who loved us and washed us from our sins in His own blood, and has made us kings and priests to His God and Father, to Him be glory and dominion forever and ever, Amen.*

Jesus loved us so much that he washed us from our sins in His own blood. If we accept this, Jesus has made us priests to

God. We are the priests in the new covenant as long as we obey the conditions. No more do we have to come from a certain tribe; we get the privilege of being priests if we accept Jesus and all He did for us. That's great news! It means that we can talk to God at any time, for the curtain that prevented the priests from going into the Holy of Holies was torn on the day Jesus died. It tells us this in Matthew 27:51:

> *Then, behold, the veil of the temple was torn in two from top to bottom; and the earth quaked, and the rocks were split.*

This opened up access to the presence of God for all those who are saved—those who have been ordained by Jesus to be priests. We can now come before God. There's no mediator anymore—we have a God we can talk to any time. We don't have to push through crowds, wait a year or wait until Jesus comes to town, our access to the throne has been thrown wide open. Hallelujah!

We need to recognise and walk in the role that Jesus has given us. It's a privilege and cost Jesus everything.

Let's pray as we close this chapter.

> *Father, we thank you that we can now enter Your presence anytime. We don't have to wait for an invitation or the right time, as the invitation has already gone out. We just have to accept that Jesus, as our High Priest, satisfied all the requirements and open our hearts and accept Him. Thank You that we are part of the*

new covenant, where our main purpose is to love God and love others. It is a great honour that You have bestowed this privilege on us. Help us to walk in all You have for us. In Jesus' name, amen.

Chapter 8—The Wilderness: The Battle for Trust in God

Now we get to the interesting part of the journey with the Israelites. So far, God has saved them, baptised them, provided for them, set them up with a structure of worship, made a covenant with them and set out the requirements, advised them on how to construct a temple and its furnishings as a place to meet with God and gave them a position and gifts. It seems that God has been doing all the work. All the Israelites had to do was agree with God's plan. So far, so good.

But what happens when life takes an unexpected turn? As the Israelites found out and what we as Christians should know is that we still have an enemy out there who wants to fight us. This enemy fights us on two fronts—one is to diminish the power and sovereignty of God in our lives and the other is to demote us or make us doubt the love of God and the position where He's placed us. If he can do that, then we start to doubt God's existence and care for us and that our salvation is real. We can then make a choice and walk away. But that's not keeping our part of the covenant, which we discussed in the last two chapters.

What lessons can we learn from the Israelites so we can recognise these tactics and stop them in our own lives? Let's keep going with our journey.

The Battle of Who God is

The first story centres around who God is in our lives. In Exodus 32, Moses was called up to the mountain to receive the

Ten Commandments, the regulations concerning all aspects of life and the design of the tabernacle and all its furnishings, including the clothing for the high priest and priests. Whilst he was up there, the Israelites became tired of waiting for him.

Moses had been on the mountain for 40 days and 40 nights—about one month and a week and a half. The Israelites didn't have mobile phones so they couldn't call Moses to see if he was okay. So they thought the worst and thought something had happened to him. The only one who continued to wait was Joshua.

The Israelites came up with a plan to build their own gods to go further on the journey with them. This is interesting. Did they think Moses was their god or that Moses was the only one who could hear from God? They made Aaron their leader and advised him to build a golden calf and in doing so, reduced the Almighty God to something they could physically touch. It tells us this in Exodus 32 verse 4:

> *And he received the gold from their hand, and he fashioned it with an engraving tool, and made a molded calf. Then they said, "This is your god, O Israel, that brought you out of the land of Egypt."*

Then the Israelites rose early to offer burnt offerings and peace offerings, but the consequences were never going to be great. Never once did they consult with God, they just went their own way.

As a result, God told Moses He was going to destroy the Israelites and make a nation out of the line of Moses. But Moses pleaded with God not to destroy them by reminding God He was compassionate and had brought the Israelites out of Egypt by His great power and with a mighty hand (verse 11). God relented and Moses returned to the people.

On returning to the people, Moses became angry and broke the tablets God had written on. He then commanded the Israelites to choose between God and themselves. The ones who chose God continued on the journey and God killed those who didn't.

This was a sad day in the camp of the Israelites. After all they had been through and all that they had seen God do, how He had delivered them time and time again, they chose to turn their backs on a spiritual God and make Him a natural god because of impatience.

How many times do we reduce God to what we can see and touch in our natural circumstances? God isn't limited by our natural circumstances in what He can do for us. God is supernatural and operates outside this world—in His Kingdom and under His principles. That's why faith is so important for us. Faith is believing God can do it, whatever 'it' is for you. It may be a financial breakthrough, healing or restoration of relationships. In the natural, it looks impossible, but with God, all things are possible.

I love what God says about Himself to Abraham and Sarah in Genesis 18:14:

Is anything too hard for the Lord?

The answer to that question is no if we believe in a supernatural God through the eyes of faith. Hebrews 11:6 tells us it's impossible to please God if we don't have faith. Faith, in Hebrews 11:1, is 'the substance of things hoped for, the evidence of things not seen'. It's a supernatural force that allows us to connect with God on a supernatural level.

This is the same as being baptised in the Holy Spirit. We are then able to pray in an unknown language and connect with God in the supernatural. 1 Corinthians 14:2 tells us:

> *For he who speaks in a tongue does not speak to*
> *men but to God, for no one understands Him;*
> *however, in the spirit He speaks mysteries.*

Mysteries to whom? Satan doesn't know what you're praying and sometimes, neither do you. But God knows and can answer your prayers. It connects you on a supernatural basis.

Don't reduce God to your natural circumstances. Always remember He's spiritual and not of this world. He operates in a different kingdom. To touch the heart of God, we must learn to honour Him and operate out of this kingdom too.

The Battle of God Going With Us

Sometimes in our lives, we don't consciously recognise the presence of God or we find ourselves in situations or in places where God wouldn't want us to go. So we leave God behind, or so we think. We forget about God's presence being with us at all times. Sometime later, we find ourselves in a place where we feel that God has forgotten us. The Bible states in Deuteronomy 31:6b:

> *"God will never leave you nor forsake you."*

If God says He will never leave us, is that true even if we don't feel the presence of God?

The Israelites found themselves in this situation in Exodus 33. God told Moses that the Israelites could go to the Promised Land without Him—that He would send His angel instead because the Israelites refused to believe in God.

Unbelief always puts us in the position of feeling like we're on our own. God is never far from us and wouldn't have been far from the Israelites either, as verse 2 states:

> *And I will send My Angel before you and I will drive out the Canaanite and the Amorite and the Hittite and the Perizzite and the Hivite and the Jebusite. Go up to a land flowing with milk and honey; for I will not go up in your midst.*

God would still be with them but from a distance. Sin and unbelief separate us from a loving God, not because God wants to leave us, but because we walk further from God.

In James 4:8a, it tells us:

> *Draw near to God, and He will draw near to you.*

This verse is interesting as there's an expectation that we will draw near to God before He draws near to us. I have heard it said many times that the Holy Spirit is a gentleman—He won't draw near unless He's invited. The same thing with God (Who the Holy Spirit is part of)—He will only draw near if we want Him to. That's the reason He created us with free will or a choice. Do we choose to walk with God or not?

When we choose not to have God be intimately connected with our everyday lives, He won't be, but we'll wonder why the blessings and favour of God aren't abounding in our lives. When we choose to walk with God intimately, we have that connection.

I was reading my Bible the other day and came across this verse (which I have probably read a number of times before). It's found in Hosea 2:16 and states:

> *"And it shall be, in that day," says the Lord, "that you will call Me My Husband, and no longer call Me My Master."*

This is what God requires. He's our Lord and not our master. The difference between the two is that one is because of love and the other is because of obligation.

God didn't want to go with the Israelites because of obligation, He wanted to go with them because they loved Him.

I love what Moses did next. He told God in Exodus 33:15:

> *"If Your Presence does not go with us, do not bring us up from here.["]*

Moses realised that without the presence of God, the people would be like any other nation, with gods that couldn't speak or hear. There would be no distinction and therefore, nothing that separated them from the other nations. They needed God to lead them, guide them and show them His grace.

Without an intimate relationship with God, we can find ourselves in the same scenario. We will talk, act and be like those around us. Our lights won't shine because God is too far away from us. Darkness will come around our lives and we will lose our way.

Like the Israelites, we must continue to have God and His presence go with us as we walk the journey of life. We can't afford not to have God walk with us. Without Him, there are no blessings, no favour, no hope and basically, no point. But with God, there's a purpose and a plan that we are walking to fulfil.

Determine in your hearts today that you will walk with God. This is a battle we must face daily against our flesh. Our flesh wants to walk its own way, but our spirit always wants to walk with God.

The Battle of Giving

Earlier in this book, we talked about the principle of tithing. The following story talks about the Israelites' heart for giving an offering to the cause. This story doesn't really speak of the battle of giving for the Israelites' sake, but I want to mention it here because it's one of the battles we face in our lives—the battle to surrender our finances to God.

The story is found in Exodus 35:4–9 and 36:2–7. The plans had been laid out for the tabernacle, the furnishings, the priests' clothing and all other items to be used in the tabernacle. However, there was a problem. Moses couldn't go to the nearest bank and ask for a loan, nor could he ask the Israelites for money to purchase the items because there were no shops. But what he could ask for was materials to build the things that were required.

In Chapter 35, Moses asks for an offering but in doing so, he laid out a number of requirements for the person making the offering. They were:

1. They had to be of a willing heart. It had to be a willing offering, not an unwilling one, and certainly not an offering just to keep up with the Joneses (whoever they are).

2. They had to bring the offering. There was a

requirement on the person to get up from where they were, walk out of their house and go to the place of giving. Each step they may have been thinking about why they should keep whatever it was. For example, 'Ruth may be cold if we don't keep this animal skin.'

3. The offering had to be specific to the requirements. God always wants us to bring a specific offering—one that's chosen beforehand and not impulsively given later.

I love what chapter 36:5 says, which is:

> *[A]nd they spoke to Moses, saying, "The people bring much more than enough for the service of the work which the Lord commanded us to do."*

And in verse 6b, it states:

> *And the people were restrained from bringing.*

I don't know about you, but I have never been in a church or a guest ministry meeting where the pastors have told the congregation to stop giving because they had enough. Generally, it's the other way around. One day, I would like to experience it (even if it's just once).

So what does this story have to do with our giving? We're already giving tithes, what more does God expect? That can be summed up in one word—generosity. God wants us to be moved to give by compassion and not by someone tying our hands behind our backs.

God is a generous God. He gave up all He had—His only Son, Jesus, to die on the cross for us so we could be restored and the Holy Spirit, who is now down on earth with us, instead of in heaven.

God doesn't expect us to put all our wages or income into the bucket on Sunday, but He expects us to have a generous heart. When there's a special offering at your church or a ministry that's on your heart, you need to give with the principles that have been outlined above:

- Have a willing heart and bring your offering
- Determine what the requirements are and give accordingly

Sometimes in church, we're asked to give finances, pancake shakers for end-of-school celebrations, icy poles for beginning-of-university-year celebrations, clothing and blankets for homeless people or our time and food to feed the homeless and needy.

There are many ways you can be involved in giving, but there's a battle going on. Satan doesn't want you to give, he wants you to hoard. Many times, we don't give out of fear that we won't have enough, but I love the scripture in Philippians 4:19 where it says:

> *And my God shall supply all your need*
> *according to His riches in glory by Christ Jesus.*

We quote this verse often over all our circumstances, but this scripture was birthed out of the Philippian church giving to the Apostle Paul's needs time and again. This scripture was not birthed out of tithing, but out of offerings.

It's time for us to trust God and give, not to get, but to be a blessing, and not out of fear, but out of complete trust in our Heavenly Father. The battle will only rage in your mind whilst the offering is still in your hands. Once you have given, it's God's battle to see that your needs are met and He always wins.

The Battle for Honour

Honour seems like such a gallant word, as we usually associate it with war and winning some great battle. But honour is a term that's used to describe the relationship that one has either between persons or between a person and their god. In the *Pocket Oxford Dictionary*, honour is described as glory, high reputation and exalted position. For Christians, we honour God or grant Him an exalted position in our lives because He is our creator, redeemer, Saviour and Lord. God is already in this exalted position, but we must choose to put Him in this place in our lives as a mark of respect.

However, due to our flesh nature (the natural part of us that wants everything for self), this is a battle that we sometimes face regularly. Our flesh wants to do its own thing, whereas our redeemed spirit wants to do it God's way. Our spirit wants to pray and read the Bible, but our flesh wants to watch television and look at Facebook.

The Israelites had this same issue and we're going to consider the story in Leviticus 10:1–3. It is only a short story, but it shows the concept of honouring God in everything. The story centres on Aaron's (the high priest) sons, Nadab and Abihu. Nadab and Abihu had been chosen as priests to serve with their father, Aaron, in the temple of God. It was a privilege to serve God in this way as none of the other Israelites had been given this privilege (only the four sons of Aaron, at this stage).

Instead of considering it a privilege, they decided to take some liberties. In Exodus 30:9, God commanded that Aaron (the high priest) should burn incense on the Altar of Incense only at twilight every day when he lit the lamps. The incense had to be made using a special formula (described in verses 34–38 of the same chapter). Aaron was commanded not to burn strange incense, a burnt offering, a grain offering or a drink offering on the Altar of Incense. It was to be used for one purpose only.

Nadab and Abihu decided to disobey that commandment and offered profane fire on the Altar of Incense. As a result, fire came out and they died before the altar. Their decision to not obey the commandments regarding the presence of God and therefore, not honouring God, had devastating results for these men.

God takes honour very seriously and so should we. We need to honour the things of God and the presence of God in our daily lives. We should not treat church as common but as holy ground, every time we step into it.

In the New Testament, the word we translate as 'church' is *ecclesia*, which means the assembly of citizens. The Bible further expands on this to mean the whole body of Christians and the local church where a company of Christians gathers for worship, sharing and teaching. This means that we should also honour each other as we are the Church (not the building).

Who else does the Bible command us to honour? In Matthew 15:4, it says to honour our father and mother. 1 Peter 2:17 tells us to honour all people and the king (our president, prime minister, premier, etc). Honour does not mean always agreeing, but it means to recognise the role and hold it in high esteem.

The battle to honour God or others is always tough but it is doable. God raises leaders and pulls them down. Our role is to love and honour God and love and honour others. By doing so, the blessings will flow and the favour of God will be upon our lives.

Let's pray:

> *Father, we ask you to help us honour You and others. Show us areas in our lives where we are not honouring. We repent of this sin in our lives; please forgive us. Help us to honour You more and more and honour others too. In Jesus' name, amen.*

The Battle of Complaining

Complaining—we hear so much about it. What is it really? The *Pocket Oxford Dictionary* meaning for 'complain' is 'make a statement that one is aggrieved or dissatisfied with one who is in authority'. This is a pretty harsh meaning for a word. No wonder God hates complainers. In Jude 15–16, complainers are listed with those who speak harsh words about God.

Why does God hate complaining so much? It's because when we complain, it tells God we're dissatisfied or aggrieved with something happening in our life. Is everything that happens in our lives God's fault? No, of course not! But that's sometimes who we blame if things go wrong in our lives. God seems an easy target as we can shift responsibility for our lives and our actions on One who could have stopped it. Bad things happening in our lives don't come from God. James 1:17 states:

> *Every good gift and every perfect gift is from above, and comes down from the Father of*

> *lights, with whom there is no variation or*
> *shadow of turning.*

This is an important verse to meditate on. God only gives good and perfect gifts and not bad ones. He's not controlled by how good we've been or how much time we've spent with Him. There's no variation in God's will as to who those good and perfect gifts go to. So why complain? Take your requests to God and wait for your answer. It's the best solution to your problems and issues. The problem is that we can't wait. We want a microwave God. It's not going to happen.

So what happens when we complain? Let's go back to our journey with the Israelites in Numbers 11:1–2:

> *Now when the people complained, it displeased*
> *the Lord; for the Lord heard it, and His anger*
> *was aroused. So the fire of the Lord burned*
> *among them, and consumed some on the*
> *outskirts of the camp. Then the people cried out*
> *to Moses, and when Moses prayed to the Lord,*
> *the fire was quenched.*

This is not the usual story in the Israelites' journey as it is one instance, but very generic. We don't know what they were complaining about but whatever it was, it captured God's attention. Let's look at these verses in detail to see what we can learn.

The first thing is that God heard them complaining. If you think God doesn't listen to what you say, you're wrong. God hears every word that we speak and that's why we must be careful what we say because every idle word will be judged.

God's anger was aroused. Why? The solution is to stop complaining and take our concerns to God. As stated before, if we complain about something, we aren't trusting in God to handle our situations. That's the reason He gets angry.

For example, you have a child that you love very dearly. You provide shelter, food, clothing, love and everything else the child requires. You do your best to ensure that child is protected and cared for.

One day, however, your child starts complaining to you about how he/she doesn't like the food you're cooking and furthermore, they don't like the bed they sleep in and their clothes are out of date and not good enough.

How would you react? I would be hurt and also a little angry. Why? I have poured my life and resources into this child and have provided anything they needed but they didn't tell me they didn't like carrots and didn't like wearing their old clothes to school on free dress day. If they had communicated this, the issues would have been sorted without complaining.

Do you see what I mean when I say God gets upset with us? We complain but we don't come to Him first. In essence, we're blaming God for our troubles.

The second point I want you to consider was that the fire consumed those on the outskirts of the camp. The tabernacle was in the middle. These complainers were on the edge.

If we get too far away from God, we start to complain, as we aren't near Him. God is never far away from us because He said that He will never leave us or forsake us. We move away from God. There can be many reasons for this. For example, it might be guilt that we have done or said something that's displeasing to God, or that other things have taken priority in our lives and we feel God is too far away. Or perhaps a circumstance has made us forget the goodness of God.

When you and I are facing these types of things, we need to run to God and not away from Him. Even if you don't feel like going to church, go. If you don't feel like singing, sing. If you don't feel like reading the Bible, read one verse. If you don't feel like praying, pray two sentences. God will meet you where you are but only if you run to Him. Don't complain, run to the One who loves you dearly.

Let's pray:

> *God, we thank you that you are always with us. We are the ones who lose our way with You. We have been caught in the cycle of complaining instead of running to You, who we trust. Please forgive us. As we draw closer to You, please draw close to us. Remind us of how much You love and care for us. God, we love You and praise You. In Jesus' name, amen.*

The Battle of Craving

Craving is usually a battle with food so it is in the story in Numbers 11:4–35. However, craving can occur in our lives in a number of different ways and we'll consider them once we've looked at our story.

First, what's the meaning of 'craving'? In the *Pocket Oxford Dictionary*, it means 'a strong desire'. It may not be about food only. Let's look at the story and see what God thinks about it.

In verses 4–6, it states:

> *Now the mixed multitude who were among them*
> *yielded to intense [lusted intensely] craving; so*
> *the children of Israel also wept again and said:*
> *"Who will give us meat to eat? We remember the*
> *fish which we ate freely in Egypt, the cucumbers,*
> *the melons, the leeks, the onions and the garlic; but*
> *now our whole being is dried up; there is nothing at*
> *all except this manna before our eyes!"*

There are a couple of points to focus on in these verses.

1. It was first the mixed multitude who yielded to this craving – this strong desire to eat something other than manna. This is interesting to me. It wasn't the Israelites that complained first, it was the mixed multitude that came out of Egypt or inter-relationships that occurred between the Egyptians and the Israelites. People who aren't close to God will always have a strong desire to do something against Him. Why? They sit either over the fence or on the fence of their Christianity and are tempted more easily because they are further away from the vine. It's easy to become disconnected from God when the world and circumstances around us are trying to creep in. It's similar to the story of Peter walking on the water. As long as he had his eyes on Jesus, he was okay, but as soon as he took his eyes off Jesus, he started to sink. The world promises many things and it's easy to get caught up in the strong desires of the world. 1 John 2:16 gives us the base for what the strong desires of the world look like:

> *For all that is in the world—the lust of the*
> *flesh, the lust of the eyes, and the pride of life—*
> *is not of the Father but is of the world.*

Be careful of the world around you. It will tempt you with those strong desires.

2. The Israelites wanted to know who would give them meat to eat. It's interesting that in the next sentence, the only meat that's mentioned is fish and the rest were vegetables (which I could give or take; don't know about you). So this seems like a smokescreen. A smokescreen is something hiding the real reason for the upset. What were they upset about? The choice of food, which was limited to manna.

3. Manna was God's food from heaven. It was food not only to sustain them but also to prove their trust in God. By despising the manna, they were despising their trust in God. They were telling God He wasn't good enough to meet their needs and desires.

Let's think about these points for a minute. Can you think of some things in your life where the craving for something other than God has taken over? I can. I wanted to play Candy Crush on my iPad. I loved the thrill of the challenge of the mind and my analytical skills. It was easy to play at first, but then I got to the stage where it was taking over everything. I wanted desperately to win the next level. I tried to convince myself that if I just won the game for the day, then that would be it. The problem was the higher the level, the harder it was to win easily.

It took over my life for a few weeks. However, I realised I had to let it go and delete it from my iPad so it would lose the hold it had over my life.

Did it work? It did but only after the second or third time of deleting it from my iPad. Things like games aren't bad but when they take over your life and you get a strong desire to play them continually, they aren't good.

There's a verse in Hebrews 12:1 that sums this up well. It states:

> *Therefore we also, since we are surrounded by so great a cloud of witnesses, let us lay aside every weight, and the sin which so easily ensnares us, and let us run with endurance the race that is set before us.*

Craving causes us to lose our desire for the race that God has set before us. It causes us to fix our minds on the craving and not on the race.

Each of us has the same battle with craving, but different battles with the desires themselves. Some might desire television, others sports, movies, food, acceptance, popularity, riches, climbing the corporate ladder (no matter who you step on in the process), etc. The list can be long.

It doesn't matter what your craving is, the outcome is the same—it will take you further from God and further from His purpose and plan for your life. Do you want to risk it? I don't, but this is a major battle for me at times. Run to God and not away from Him and let Him help you break its hold over your life. You're worth far more to God and God's plan is worth far more than your craving.

So what happened to the Israelites? It affected Moses first and we'll look at the battle of responsibility in the next section. We need to skip down to Numbers 11:31–35 to find out what happened.

God answered their craving for meat but the consequences of it were not good. Let's see what happened in verses 32–33:

> *And the people stayed up all that day, all night, and all the next day, and gathered the quail (he who gathered least gathered 10 homers); and they spread them out for themselves all around the camp. But while the meat was still between their teeth, before it was chewed, the wrath of the Lord was aroused against the people, and the Lord struck the people with a very great plague.*

Verse 34 states that they buried the people who had yielded to craving. Craving is a very dangerous thing. It takes us out of the will of God and out of His purpose. It also tells God we don't trust Him.

What should the Israelites and we do instead? Go to God and tell him our hearts. Repent of our craving and ask Him to remove the stronghold. The manna represented the Bread of Life, which is Jesus and He's all we need in this life. He promised to provide everything for us as long as we put the Kingdom of God in first place in our lives.

The Kingdom of God is righteousness, peace and joy in the Holy Ghost. Our lives need to consist of right living before God, with nothing missing and nothing broken in our lives and love in our hearts for God, others and ourselves. If we live this way, we won't need to crave what the world offers.

Let's pray:

> *Father, we come to you and repent of the cravings that are in our lives. We ask You to help us remove those strongholds. Lord, we need our lives to be right before You, to have nothing missing and nothing broken and a love for You, others and ourselves that gives us no time for craving. Please hear our prayers and help us, Lord. In Jesus' name, amen.*

Chapter 9— The Wilderness: The Battle of Leading

The previous chapter was all about battles with our trust in God. This chapter will be all about the battle between leadership and control.

God set leaders in place in our lives. How we treat our leaders and how we control ourselves is vital to us honouring God. If we don't honour our leaders, then we are implying by our actions or thoughts that we're not honouring God because He put them in place.

None of us wants to be in that position so let's find out how we can overcome these battles.

Battle of Responsibility

Responsibility is a word that most of us think we have but once it becomes overwhelming, we want to back away from it. The word speaks of others' needs rather than our own and oftentimes their needs are too much for us to bear. In the *Pocket Oxford Dictionary*, 'responsibility' means 'being responsible or being called to account, answerable to someone and morally accountable for actions'.

In thinking about the position God gave Moses in our story, it seems like it would have been an exceedingly responsible one. Moses was in charge of getting in excess of one million people—men, women and children—into the Promised Land. It was his responsibility to ensure that all complied with the commandments and regulations and that all arrived safely. That's a big responsibility for one person and that position would become overwhelming except for one thing—Moses was only responsible to Almighty God.

That should have made it easier because God knows everything, right? Yes, if he didn't let the people's complaining wear him down. That's what happened in the story in Numbers 11:10–30. In this story, Moses heard the people weeping and was displeased. However, instead of complaining to Aaron or some other person, Moses took his complaints directly to God. This action is what God requires of us when something displeases us (as mentioned earlier in the Battle of Complaining).

The first thing we need to know about responsibility is who we are responsible to. Moses was responsible to God.

The second thing is our role in that responsibility. Are we there to lead and guide people or are we there to ensure that everything goes right all the time? The second one is hard to do as we can't be responsible for other people's thoughts and actions (unless we have done something incorrect). For example, if Moses had disobeyed God and the people followed that disobedience, then Moses would have been at fault.

I believe that Moses' responsibility was to lead and guide the people into the Promised Land. This wasn't his role at first—God only told Moses that He wanted His people to go to a specific place and worship Him. However, as the story went on, Moses' role changed in accordance with the plans and purposes of God for all His people. Moses could never be held responsible for the people's actions if they chose to disobey what He told them. Each was responsible for his own actions.

Let's look at Moses' reaction in verse 10. It states:

> *Then Moses heard the people weeping*

> *throughout their families, everyone at the door*
> *of his tent; and the anger of the Lord was greatly*
> *aroused; Moses also was displeased.*

Moses then complained to the Lord in verses 11–15 but I want to look specifically at verses 14–15, which state:

> *"I am not able to bear all these people alone,*
> *because the burden is too heavy for me. If*
> *you treat me like this, please kill me here and*
> *now—if I have found favour in Your sight—*
> *and do not let me see my wretchedness."*

We see in these verses that Moses was carrying all the responsibility by himself and therein was his battle in relation to responsibility. Moses asked God if he'd conceive these people, why hadn't he found favour in God's sight and where was he to get meat to feed all of them? Moses was bearing the whole of the responsibility by himself and this is never a good place to be in.

He was trying to please the people, rather than take time to get an answer from God. How often have we done this in our own lives? I know as a middle manager, I have done this heaps of times. We get so down that we don't run to God, we 'run away' or hide from God as pride gets in and we think we have to handle it all on our own.

Moses went into a state of depression and anxiety. That's what the battle of responsibility can do in our lives. I know, as a few years ago, I had four months off work with anxiety. I let the responsibilities of my position and pleasing people get in the way of taking all my burdens to God and letting Him speak wisdom into my life. Maybe you have felt the same.

Let's read further and see what God's answer was. In verses 16–17, God spoke to Moses and stated:

> *"Gather to Me seventy elders of Israel, whom*
> *you know to be the elders of the people and*
> *officers over them; bring them to the tabernacle*
> *of meeting, that they may stand there with you.*
> *Then I will come down and talk with you there.*
> *I will take of the Spirit that is upon you and will*
> *put the same upon them; and they shall bear the*
> *burden of the people with you, that you may not*
> *bear it yourself alone."*

God's reaction to Moses' predicament is interesting. He didn't respond to Moses' emotions but responded to the issue at hand. God will do the same with us—He doesn't respond to emotions, He responds to the issue, but better than that, is that God responds to our faith and trust in Him.

Moses went to find those 70 elders. He knew who they were. Remember the story of Jethro and Moses in Exodus 18? Jethro told Moses to appoint judges to help in judging the people. But Moses had somehow forgotten that or limited the judges' responsibility to only judging and not being men he could rely on to carry other burdens.

All too often, that's the same with us. God has already given us people around us who can help us carry the responsibility but oftentimes we don't want their help because of pride. You need to take advantage of what God has already given you. Some of those people might be your co-workers, your managers, your pastors and your trusted friends. You will know who can help you. You just have to ask.

The battle of responsibility is all to do with pride. God wants us to get rid of that pride and just do what He has called us to do wherever He has placed us, whether that is in a workplace, a school, a ministry or in your family. Every single person carries a level of responsibility (except if you're a baby).

Let's pray that this battle of responsibility won't get too overwhelming before we run to God and others for help.

> *Father, we come to you in the name of Jesus and repent of our pride in taking on the battle of responsibility. Please show us who is around to help us and give us Your wisdom and Your grace to get through the current issues. We trust you God and love you as our Daddy. In Jesus' name, amen.*

Battle of the Honour of Leadership

One of the hardest things to do in our Christian walk, at times, is to honour the leadership that God has entrusted over us. You might think, 'But I love my pastors.' That's great! But what about government leaders, your work leadership, the principal at your or your child's school, etc? God requires that we honour all our leaders, as shown in 1 Peter 2:13–18. In parts, it states:

> *Therefore submit yourselves to every ordinance (institution) of man for the Lord's sake, whether to the king as supreme, or to governors ... For this is the will of God ... Honour all people. Love*

> *the brotherhood. Fear God. Honor the King.*
> *Servants, be submissive to your masters ...*

These five verses cover honour well from God to our government leaders to our employers to our teachers.

The Israelites had the same issue with honouring their leaders, although in the story in Numbers 12, it had a bit of a different twist, or did it? Let's refresh ourselves on the leadership structure of the Israelites. Moses was appointed by God to lead the Israelites and Aaron was appointed by God as high priest. Miriam, their sister, was also in this story. She was the one who enabled Moses to be rescued and brought up in Pharaoh's palace and later on, led the praise when the Israelites crossed the Red Sea.

Miriam and Aaron spoke out against Moses' leadership and relationship with God because Moses had married a foreign woman (not an Israelite woman). Where he would have found one in the wilderness is beyond me. In verse 2, they said:

> *"Has the Lord indeed spoken only through*
> *Moses? Has He not spoken through us also?"*
> *And the Lord heard it.*

The issue was not that Moses had married a foreign woman but that God had chosen him to be the leader of the Israelites in spite of this. Why did they think they could speak out against Moses this way? It was because they were family. Familiarity brings a sense of dishonour if we allow it to. In this case, it was caused by them thinking they were entitled to the same benefits from God because they were close to Moses.

The meaning of 'familiarity' in the *Pocket Oxford Dictionary* is 'to make common with a person or to treat that person as common'. If we are familiar with someone, our actions and behaviour around that person are different from the way they are around someone we're not familiar with.

This is common in children. When my boys were younger, they were polite and well-mannered outside home but as soon as they entered our door, it was like their masks came off and they were able to relax and be themselves. Home was familiar to them, so they behaved accordingly. They were still great but their masks had fallen a bit.

Aaron and Miriam were familiar with Moses, as he was their brother. They didn't honour him in his leadership position but caused the familiarity to move across into that position. They couldn't distinguish between the familiar person and the appointed position.

God heard their complaint and came down in a pillar of cloud to investigate what was happening. He took Aaron and Miriam back to the position that He had given Moses by telling them that Moses was more than a prophet because God didn't only speak to him in dreams, but face to face. He spoke about the root cause and in part stated:

> *"And he [Moses] sees the form of the Lord. Why then were you not afraid to speak against My servant Moses?"*

God reminded them of Moses' position—he was God's servant, not just their brother.

This can happen to us in our lives also. We can become so friendly with our pastors that we forget that God has placed them in leadership over us. So when they pastor us, we can oftentimes feel hurt and offended because we have allowed that familiarity to creep in.

How do we stop this? By separating the person from the position. We must recognise the responsibility that person has over our lives and honour the position God has placed them in. With leadership also comes responsibility, as discussed earlier. However, there is a time for honour and a time for friends. If your pastor is in the pulpit sharing a message, you honour him as your pastor. If your pastor and his family are on a picnic with you and your family, there is a time for friendship, but the position is still there.

What does God think about dishonouring the position of leadership? In verse 9, it states that the anger of the Lord was aroused against Aaron and Miriam. God takes dishonouring the position of leadership very seriously.

What happened to them? Miriam contracted leprosy. Leprosy in the Bible represents sin. Aaron had to humble himself and ask Moses to pray for them. Moses prayed and God told Miriam she had to do as normal lepers did—be shut out of the camp for seven days. She was shut out from her family, from God and others.

If you have dishonoured the leadership over you, repent and ask God to forgive you. After seven days, Miriam was restored to the camp and God will do the same for you. He will restore you to the rightful place with Him.

Let's pray:

> *Father, we thank you that you have entrusted leadership over us to guide us and protect us. Please forgive us when we have dishonoured the leadership in our lives. Help us to clearly see the*

> *role that leadership of others has in our lives*
> *and please help us to submit to the direction*
> *of the leadership, even when we can't see what*
> *they're doing. Father, we put our trust in You*
> *that You will always be with us. In Jesus' name,*
> *amen.*

Battle of Unbelief

The battle of unbelief is one that we all constantly face. Unbelief comes when we don't have the faith to believe that what God says He will do, He will actually do. Faith is the opposite of unbelief and the Bible speaks much about these subjects. Let's see why before we get into our story.

Hebrews 11:6 tells us what happens when we are in unbelief:

> *But without faith it is impossible to please Him*
> *[God], for he who comes to God must believe that*
> *He is, and that He is a rewarder of those who*
> *diligently seek Him.*

If we are in unbelief, we aren't pleasing God and that's not a place a child of God wants to find themselves in. Just imagine for a moment, as a parent, if you told your child something and they didn't believe you. How does that make you feel? We would feel hurt and disrespected. Children may not see how something will affect them or that they're going down the wrong track, but as their parents, we can see it, so we try to train them and warn them. It's the same with God—He wants us to have faith in Him because He can see the bigger picture, whereas we can't.

We must come to God believing that He is what? Our creator, our redeemer, the one who sent our Saviour, the one who loves us unconditionally and the one who has come to give us life and life more abundantly. We must also believe that He rewards those who diligently seek Him. How do we do that? By reading the Bible, spending time with God and spending time with other Christians being taught the Word of God.

Now that the foundation has been laid, let's look at the story in Numbers 13 and 14. In this story, the Israelites had arrived at the edge of the Promised Land in the Wilderness of Paran. Numbers 13:1–2 tell us what happened next:

> *And the Lord spoke to Moses, saying, "Send the men to spy out the land of Canaan, which I am giving to the children of Israel; from each tribe of their fathers you shall send a man, every one a leader among them."*

God wanted the leaders of the Israelites to 'see' the Promised Land first and be able to come back and tell the people that everything God had promised them was in this land. Note that God wanted the leaders to go. This is significant, as generally, the leadership sets the direction for our lives. If the leadership can't 'see' God's promises, then they don't pass them on to their teams or their people.

God also wanted a leader from each tribe of Israel chosen so there would be no favouritism shown and all the tribes of Israel would be well-represented. So 12 men were sent out.

There was no issue with this, so Moses sent them out. If you do a study on the names of the leaders Moses sent out, you'll find their names means good things. This is significant a bit later in the story.

Those men went on a 'spy' journey throughout the Promised Land for 40 days. They brought back a branch with one cluster of grapes on it that was so big two of them had to carry it on a pole, some figs and pomegranates. In other words, it was the natural fruit and provision that the land had to offer. Let's look at their report about the Promised Land in verses 27–29 of Numbers 13. They said:

> *"We went to the land where you sent us. It truly flows with milk and honey, and this is its fruit. Nevertheless the people who dwell in the land are strong; the cities are fortified and very large; moreover we saw the descendants of Anak there. The Amalekites dwell in the land of the South; the Hittites, the Jebusites, and the Amorites dwell in the mountains; and the Canaanites dwell by the sea, and along the banks of the Jordan."*

Before we go further with the story, let's have a look at their report. There are two lines of good and six lines of bad. The first good line is 'we went to the land where you sent us'—God had fulfilled His promise to bring them to the land. The second good line is 'it truly flows with milk and honey'—God had fulfilled His promise to bring them to the land flowing with milk and honey. This is great—God's promises are all fulfilled. However, there is a 'but' moment. 'But" moments are where our belief in God is tested.

So what was the Israelites 'but' moment? They had already defeated some of their enemies, so what was wrong? The last six lines—the enemies were strong, their cities are fortified and very large and they are everywhere they looked. Our unbelief moments come when the enemy looks stronger, bigger and appears all around us. We aren't focused on the goodness and the promises of God anymore. We're focused on whatever enemy is in front of us. Our verse in the New Testament for this is found in Mark 11: 22–23 and states:

> *"Have faith in God. For assuredly, I say unto you, whoever says to this mountain, 'Be removed and be cast in to the sea', and does not doubt in his heart, but believes that those things he says will be done, he will have whatever he says."*

The Israelites had to go in and defeat their enemies using physical force. We defeat our enemies using our faith in God and His Word.

This has now become a bad report as the Israelites focus on the negatives and not on God. Caleb tries to turn their minds again to the power of God in Numbers13:30, but he doesn't succeed.

Unbelief leads to fear and an unwillingness to believe in the promises of God. The 10 spies continued with their bad report and turned the Israelites from the promise of God. Their unbelief caused them to eventually see themselves in the supposed minds of their enemies.

This is found in verse 33:

> *"There we saw the giants ... and we were like grasshoppers in our own sight, and so we were in their sight."*

Unbelief will always give us a low opinion of ourselves.

These are the Hebrew meanings of the names of the leaders who were sent to spy out the land:

Name	Meaning
Shammua	Renowned
Shaphat	Judge
Caleb	Attack
Igal	Avenger
Oshea (Joshua)	Deliverer
Palti	Delivered
Gaddiel	Fortune of God
Gaddi	Fortunate
Ammiel	People of God
Sethur	Hidden
Nahbi	Occult
Geuel	Majesty of God

Most of their names had great meanings and they were great men of God. However, something happened that caused them to doubt—what they saw with their natural eyes. To stay in belief in God, we need to see into the spiritual and see what God is doing.

Later on, after forty years wandering in the wilderness, the Israelites were able to take the Promised Land, as the people in the land were living in fear because of them. How do I know? In Joshua, we hear the story of the second lot of spies that were sent into the Promised Land, this time by Joshua. The two spies came to a place called Jericho and met a prostitute by the name of Rahab. She told them the following in Joshua 2:9–11:

> *"I know that the Lord has given you the land,
> that the terror of you has fallen on us, and that
> all the inhabitants of the land are fainthearted
> because of you. For we heard how the Lord dried
> up the water of the Red Sea for you when you
> came out of Egypt, and what you did to the two
> kings of the Amorites who were on the other side
> of the Jordan, Sihon and Og, whom you utterly
> destroyed. And as soon as we heard these things,
> our hearts melted: neither did there remain any
> more courage in anyone because of you, for the
> Lord your God, He is God in heaven above and
> on earth beneath."*

The Israelites' enemies had more faith in God than they did. It's the same with us. Our enemies (the devil and his cohorts) know the power of God sometimes more than we do. We need to keep our trust in God.

So what happened to the Israelites? They cried all night and God told them to turn around and go back into the wilderness. They weren't ready for the Promised Land. Some of them rebelled and went anyway, but they were killed and chased by the enemies. God said that all those who didn't believe and were aged 20 years old and over wouldn't go into the Promised Land but would walk around the wilderness until they died. Only Joshua and Caleb would be allowed in because they'd believed God.

We need to believe what God says. I have walked around too many mountains in my life instead of speaking to them and seeing them removed. The time is over for us to be walking around our wilderness. It's time for us to conquer our Promised Land. Let's pray:

> *God, we come to You and repent of those times in our lives we haven't believed in You and Your Word. Help us to take Your Word and obey it by applying it to our lives. Where we fall again into unbelief, show us and forgive us when we repent. Lord, we want belief in You to flood our hearts and minds. In Jesus' name, amen.*

The Battle of Rebellion Against Leaders

In this book, we have already spoken on the topic of honouring our leaders. This is a deliberate action each of us must take in our own hearts. Honour is between two people, groups of people or between God and us. So what happens when we involve others in our dishonouring? It becomes rebellion. To dishonour means to bring disgrace upon someone, but rebellion means an open resistance to authority—others are involved.

Note - if you are under a leader that is behaving in an ungodly manner, then you need to pray and if appropriate, remove yourself from under that person (it is not rebellion but protection). This does not give you the right to gossip to others as that will bring dishonour upon the person.

But in general, God takes rebellion against authority very seriously. That's the reason Satan was thrown out of heaven— he rebelled against the authority of God. Why is rebellion so dangerous?

God has set leaders in their places. It's His role to raise up leaders and demote them. Rebellion is us taking on God's role to demote leaders. We are getting out of order in the line of authority.

The Israelites dealt with this battle also in the wilderness. Here's the story in Numbers 16:

> *Now Korah ... with Dathan and Abiram ... and On ... took men and they rose up before Moses with some of the children of Israel, two hundred and fifty leaders of the congregation, representatives of the congregation, men of renown. They gathered together against Moses and Aaron, and said to them, "You take too much upon yourselves, for all the congregation is holy, every one of them, and the Lord is among them. Why then do you exalt yourselves above the assembly of the Lord?" So when Moses heard it, he fell on his face.*

The men spoke partial truth—the entire congregation was holy and the Lord was among them. However, partial truth always has an element of deception and wrong truth (lies). God makes all of us holy when we give our lives to Jesus, but God is a God of order and sets leadership in place according to His order.

God chose Moses and Aaron for their roles—Moses as the leader of Israel and Aaron as the high priest. They didn't ask for the roles and probably would have been content not to take them on. However, when God calls, He equips. To disobey the calling of God will lead us down wrong paths.

In Ephesians 4:11, it states:

> *And He (God) Himself gave some to be apostles,*
> *some prophets, some evangelists and some*
> *pastors and teachers.*

This is a calling from God and needs to be accepted and obeyed as such. Craving someone else's calling can be dangerous to them and us—them because they start to doubt the calling of God on their lives and us because it was never our calling in the first place.

I have struggled with this issue personally, not outwardly but inwardly. I felt for many years that God had overlooked me. My desire was to fulfil the call of God on my life but that seemed to be far off. It seemed that people newer in their walk with God were discovering their calling and walking in it, but I'd been left behind.

The truth was, I hadn't been left behind but the calling on my life just took a lot of preparation because what He'd called me to do I wasn't capable of—it's my worst skill. That's okay because now I know that whatever I do for God is all God and none of me. Some of us learn that lesson quicker than others.

What happened to those who rebelled? Moses told them that the next day God would show who He had called and who was holy. Why the next day? This would give those people time to think about what they'd said and ask for forgiveness. God is always a God of mercy and grace if we will see the situation for what it is.

On the next day, they still hadn't repented so God separated the rebellious ones and their families from the rest of the congregation. The earth opened up and swallowed them all—

them, their families and their possessions.

Rebellion against authority will not only affect us but will also affect our families.

If you have been in rebellion against leadership, it's time to pray and ask God for forgiveness. Let's pray:

> *Father, I come before You and repent of my rebellion against my leaders. I pray that I will not be jealous over their calling but realise that You have a great plan for my life. Father, I know You are no respecter of persons and that as I seek You more, You'll lead me in the direction You want me to go and on my own journey. Father, Your will be done in my life. In Jesus' name, amen.*

The Battle of Leaders' Disobedience

If you are a leader, then there are people following you. Most of us don't consider ourselves leaders because we don't have that title. In the *Pocket Oxford Dictionary*, a leader is described as 'a person followed by others'. This meaning indicates that a title isn't necessary.

What are some types of leaders in our communities? Our government leaders, school teachers, pastors, life group leaders, fathers and mothers and everyone in the Church. Why the last one? It's because once you call yourself a Christian, everyone is going to look to you, both in the Church and in the world.

Let's look first at what God says about leaders in the Bible. In 1 Peter 2:13–17, it tells us to submit to our leaders and honour the king. In verse 18, the Bible tells us to submit to our masters. Also, in 1 Timothy 2:1–2, the Bible tells us to pray for our kings and all those in authority.

What is the reason for that? It's found in Daniel 2:21:

> *And He changes the times and the seasons; He removes kings and raises up kings.*

God placed them there in the first place. Remember the story of Pharaoh and Moses? God raised up Pharaoh for His purpose and hardened his heart to remove His people from the land of Egypt.

As leaders are appointed by God, He expects them to set an example for those underneath them. This is where the next part of the journey from Egypt to the Promised Land comes in. In Numbers 20, the congregation had run out of water, so they came against Moses and Aaron in verses 2–5. Moses did what he normally did in these circumstances—he went to God and fell on his face for an answer.

In verse 8, God gave them the answer. Let's take a closer look at that verse:

> *"Take the rod; you and your brother Aaron gather the congregation together. Speak to the rock before their eyes, and it will yield its water; thus you shall bring water for them out of the rock, and give drinks to the congregation and their animals."*

Take the rod—the same rod that had been turned into a serpent and parted the Red Sea. Speak to the rock. What? No one had ever spoken to a rock before (well, maybe they had, but I doubt they expected an inanimate object to obey them). It will yield its water. This rock had been yielding water for a long time but all of a sudden it had stopped working. What's the reason for that?

We will deviate our story a little bit and explain. The rock was a representation of Jesus—He is the Living Water (John 4:10). Moses had already smitten the rock back in Exodus 17:6. Jesus was only to be smitten once for our sins, with water and blood gushing out His side (John 19:34). After that, to obtain the power from the Living Water, we have to speak the words of Jesus.

So what did Moses do? In verse 11, he struck the rock twice and water came out. But he paid a high price for disobeying God. Aaron and he were banished from ever going into the Promised Land. Moses would see the land from afar, but he would never enter it.

God always shows a natural example in the Bible for a spiritual lesson. He wanted Moses to speak to the rock so that later on, we would speak the Word ourselves, put it in our hearts so that when we needed it, it would come gushing out.

In verse 12, God spoke to Moses and told him the reason they would never enter the Promised Land:

> *"Because you did not believe Me, to hallow Me*
> *in the eyes of the children of Israel ..."*

'Hallowed' means to make the Lord holy. Leaders are meant to make the Lord holy in front of their followers. When God tells them to do something, they must do it as it not only affects them but all those who follow them. That's why the consequences are so high. That's the reason we must pray that our leaders will obey what God is telling them. If we are leaders, we need to ensure we hear and obey the Lord's direction. We need to repent when we miss the mark.

This battle is one we all face. Sometimes we don't want to look silly in front of others as sometimes God asks us to do things that are a bit unusual (eg speak to a rock). God isn't asking us to look silly; He is asking us to trust Him.

Let's pray:

> *Father, we thank You that you raise up leaders and pull leaders down. First, we come before you and repent for not honouring our leaders or praying for them as we should. Please help us to do that. Second, as we are leaders in some capacity, I pray, Father, that you will help us to obey You no matter what so we can continue to please You in all we do. We repent for any disobedience on our part as leaders. Help us to rectify any situations. In Jesus' name, amen.*

Chapter 10—The Wilderness: The Battle of Emotions

We've covered battles with our trust in God and leadership and control. Now we come to the battle with our emotions. God gave us emotions, but the key is in how we use these emotions. We need to deal with situations when they come up as God would have us deal with them.

The Battle of Rejection

Have you ever been through the battle of rejection? Most of us suffer with this at one time or another. We can be rejected by our parents (birth or adoptive), by our teachers as not being good enough, our friends, or even by ourselves (with negative self-talk).

But what does rejection really mean? In the *Pocket Oxford Dictionary*, 'reject' means 'to put aside as not to be accepted, practised, believed, chosen, used or complied with'. This seems to cover most situations in our everyday lives. But how do we overcome our battle of rejection? Let's look at the story starting in Numbers 20:14.

Moses and the Israelites had come to the nation of Edom. They wanted only to walk through the nation on the road (not in the fields or vineyards) and not strip the country of any natural resources or the people of their resources. It seemed a good deal but the King of Edom refused them twice and then came out to war against them.

What did Moses and the Israelites do? They turned away from him. They weren't going to let the rejection of the

Edomites ruin their reputation or their day. They simply just turned away. Moses could have fought them—the Israelites had conquered other nations—but he didn't. Why? We find our answer in Genesis 36:9:

> *And this is the genealogy of Esau the father of the Edomites in Mount Seir.*

Esau was the father of the Edomites. Jacob and Esau were twin brothers. God changed Jacob's name to Israel. If they hadn't walked away, they would have fought against family.

Sometimes it can be easy to turn around and walk off. The saying 'just shake it off' comes to mind. But at other times, it can be hard. What can we do?

Confess that God is love and He loves you. He'll never leave you or forsake you (Deuteronomy 31:6) and He'll never reject you. Just cry out to the One who loves you so much and He'll help you through it.

Moses never said one bad word against the Edomites. He walked in love with the Edomites, even when they didn't treat him well. That's what we must do and it's what God expects of us. Is it hard? Yes. Love isn't a feeling, it's an action.

That doesn't mean that God never judged them. He did. The Bible states that 'vengeance is mine, I will repay, says the Lord' (Romans 12:19). Isaiah 34:5 talks about the judgement of Edom from God. It states:

> *For My sword shall be bathed in heaven; Indeed it shall come down on Edom, And on the people of My curse for judgement.*

Verse 6 goes on to say, 'And a great slaughter in the land of Edom'.

If Moses and the Israelites hadn't turned away, God would have judged them. But instead, God blessed Israel and judged Edom. Sometimes, the greatest blessings in our lives come from the way we handle our greatest rejections.

I was adopted at birth and had three names in the first month of life. Rejection started right then. I battled with it for many years and still do, to a certain extent, but the stronghold of it has been broken over my life.

My first marriage ended and I was the sole provider of two boys. Three years later, I married a wonderful man who continues to this day to speak life over me. I know God loves me unconditionally, my husband loves me unconditionally and my children love me unconditionally. No one else's opinions matter because that's all they are—their opinions.

God doesn't want you to battle rejection anymore in your life. He wants to set you free to live the life God intended for you to live. Let's pray:

> *Father, I thank you that You love us*
> *unconditionally. I thank You that You sent*
> *Jesus to show us what love really looks like. We*
> *repent of the times in our lives when we thought*
> *we weren't good enough. We are good enough*
> *because You created us in your image and*
> *likeness. Help us to always remember that You*
> *love us and You will never leave us or forsake us.*
> *In Jesus' name, amen.*

The Battle of Discouragement

The next battle we will look at is discouragement. In the dictionary, this means 'reduce the confidence or spirits of or deter from'.

Have you ever had your confidence reduced? I have many times. Maybe you went to a job interview and didn't get it or maybe the guy you really liked picked someone else. Maybe you were put down your whole childhood or even as an adult and can't seem to find your way out.

Hebrews 3:6 states:

> *But Christ as a Son over His own house, whose house we are if we hold fast the confidence and the rejoicing of the hope firm to the end.*

We're God's house and exceedingly loved by Him. That should give us the confidence to hold our heads up high and know that we're a son or daughter of the King.

The Israelites had to battle the same thing in Numbers 21. Let's have a look at that story and see how they handled discouragement.

Verse 4 states that the Israelites were on a journey from Mount Hor by way of the Red Sea to go around the land of Edom and their souls became discouraged on the way. Verse 5 tells us the reason—they had no food and no water, only manna. They were getting tired of the journey, as it was taking too long. On our own journeys, if the way to where we want to go seems to take too long, we can become discouraged too. Are we ever going to get there?

We know the journey may be long for a reason but sometimes we don't want to learn the lessons required. Our confidence becomes shattered because we see others getting their dreams and it seems like we're a long way from ours.

Discouragement comes when we measure our journey in God against someone else's journey or we measure their success by our success. To go further, we need to travel longer and sometimes God has far-off destinations for us because that destination is more spectacular than others we see along the way.

Discouragement is a sin in God's eyes (Hebrews 12:1-2) because it means that we aren't trusting in Him and in His perfect plan for our lives. The Israelites learnt this lesson the hard way as snakes came into their camp, bit some of them and they died.

How did this stop? They had to make a snake, set it on a pole and when the people looked at it, they lived. When we become discouraged, we need to look to Jesus, remember what He did for us on the cross and repent.

God created you perfectly with a good plan for your life (Jeremiah 29:11). The journey might be long, but it will be worth it. To go deeper in God means you have to travel further. To find out the extent of God's love for people, you have to go wider. To touch heaven, you have to go higher. It's time for us to stop scratching in the chicken yard and soar like an eagle.

Discouragement will keep us in the chicken yard but trusting in God will enable us to soar.

Let's pray:

> *Father, forgive us for being discouraged over*
> *who you created us to be, the plans you have*
> *for our lives and how long the journey is*
> *taking. Please help us to trust in You, in Your*

> *plan for our lives and know that You love us*
> *unconditionally and will never leave us. Thank*
> *you for everything. In Jesus' name, amen.'*

The Battle of the Mouth

The next battle we will consider is sometimes the hardest of them all—the battle of the mouth.

Proverbs 18:21 tells us that death and life are in the power of the tongue, and those who love it will eat its fruit. Our mouth, through our tongue, can cause blessings and curses. These blessings and curses that come out of our mouths can be over our lives or someone else's. Blessings are beneficial and curses are destructive. Blessings can encourage but curses can discourage.

In Numbers 22, we read the story of Balak and Balaam. Israel had camped in the plains of Moab (verse 1). When Balak, the King of the Moabites saw them, he was afraid, as there was a large number of Israelites. He knew they had defeated the Amorites so it was useless sending out his army. So what was he to do instead?

He sent for Balaam. We aren't told the reason but Balaam must have had a reputation. In verse 6, Balak told his messengers that whoever Balaam blesses is blessed and whoever Balaam curses is cursed.

Balak wanted Balaam to curse the Israelites as that was the only way he knew to defeat them. Just imagine this for a minute—a powerful king knew that war and weapons weren't going to defeat this army, but words would. How powerful are our words? Have you ever thought about them in this context?

James talks about the power of words in James chapter 3. He gives us some images of what the power of words is actually like. It's a battle and possibly not one that we'll ever overcome but it must be fought minute by minute until those minutes become an hour, then hour by hour until those hours become a day, then day by day until those days become a week, then week by week until those weeks become a year and so on.

He uses the imagery of horses and ships. We put bits in horses' mouths so they obey and turn. Ships have very small rudders that assist in turning them even though they're large (James 3:3–4).

But what about our small tongue? In verse 6 it's compared to a fire—a world of iniquity or unrighteousness. It causes damage to the whole body, which we'll examine shortly. In verse 9, it talks about how it accomplishes this—we talk and bless God and then we curse men. Out of this small member comes blessings and curses and in verse 10, it says it should not be so.

So is all doomed? Definitely not, but we must allow the Holy Spirit to help us to overcome this battle. We won't do it ourselves but only with His help.

Jesus puts it this way in Matthew 15:11 when He states that what goes into the mouth doesn't defile a man but what comes out of the mouth does. Our words can tell others who we really are because they come from our hearts (verse 18). If we have bad things in our hearts, bad things will come out of our mouths and conversely, if we have good things in our hearts, good will come out of our mouths.

So how do we ensure only good things are in our hearts? Romans 12:2 tells us not to be conformed to the things of this world but to be transformed by the renewing of our minds. Our minds can only be renewed by the Word of God. For example, once we overcome anger in our hearts, angry words won't come out of our mouths.

So the process is:

1. Renew our minds with the Word of God.

2. Get God's Word in our hearts.

3. Our mouths will then speak what's in our hearts.

Is this process easy? No, it's hard and one we'll battle with for a long time, but progress will be made until one day, you'll notice your words blessing yourselves and others instead.

Let's pray:

> *Father, I pray that You'll help me in this area.*
> *Help me to have a love for the Word of God*
> *so that I'll read it and it will transform my*
> *life from the heart through the mouth to the*
> *outside, where others can see. Lord, help me set*
> *a guard over my mouth and keep watch over*
> *the door of my lips (Psalm 141:3) so that I will*
> *speak only blessings over myself and others and*
> *not curses. Thank you, Jesus. Amen.*

The Battle of the Will

We're going to digress from talking about emotions to talking about the will. Our will is still in our soul realm as our soul is made up of our mind, our will and our emotions.

There are three types of wills scattered throughout the Bible, although they're not mentioned specifically. They are the perfect will of God, the permissive will of God and not doing God's will at all. In this story, we're going to cover the first two.

In Numbers 22, we will continue with the story of Balak and Balaam. In the last section, we covered our words in relation to this story. This time I want to look at our will.

We know that Balak sent messengers to Balaam because Balak wanted Balaam to curse the Israelites. We pick the story up in verse 7. The messengers arrive at Balaam's house and advise him of the words and request that Balak has made.

So Balaam went to seek the Lord about the matter. In verse 12, we read God's response:

> *"You shall not go with them; you shall not curse the people, for they are blessed."*

So Balaam sent the messengers of Balak away with this word. This was God's perfect will for the situation. He gave the command and expected it to be carried out. It was protection for not only the Israelites (from being cursed) but also for Balaam.

But this isn't the end of the story. Balak didn't like the response so in verse 15, he sent even more princes who were more honourable and numerous than the ones before.

How did Balaam respond? Verse 18 is the response he was meant to give them which was no, but something happened in verse 19. He asked the messengers to stay the night and he would seek God again. Why would he do that? God had already given him the answer and it was no.

Do you ever catch yourself doing the same thing? We seek God about a situation and He gives us a response, which we act upon. But later, when the situation starts to heat up, we go back to God, hoping for a better response. Let me tell you from experience, God's first response is always the best response. It's for our protection and our benefit.

So Balaam went back to God and God said to go with them but only speak the words that He told him. What? Did God change His mind? One hundred percent no, but God knew that Balaam wanted to go. This is God's permissive will. He allows us to do what we want even when He says 'no', as God has given us free will.

So what happened in our story? God was angry with Balaam for going. God gave him permission, but it wasn't His perfect will. When God gives us permission that's against His will, consequences will follow.

God sent an angel to potentially kill Balaam and it would have happened, except for Balaam's donkey. The donkey saw the angel three times and moved out of its way. Balaam punished his donkey three times until the donkey spoke to him. I don't know about you, but if a donkey or any animal spoke to me, I would be in shock. But not Balaam, his anger overrode his senses.

The angel then spoke to Balaam in verse 32 and advised him that his way was contrary to God's. What was Balaam's response? In verse 34, he said:

> ["]Now therefore, if it displeases You. I will turn back."

When the will is intent on going, it can't be changed. Balaam didn't say, 'Okay I'll go back, I repent and I sinned.' No, he acknowledged that he'd sinned but would only go back if God said. He didn't really want to. We need to be careful we don't fall into the same trap. 'Okay God, I won't do this only because you don't like it.' God expects us, as Christians, to hate sin as much as He does and not make excuses for it. Disobedience to God is sin and the consequences can be severe.

Balaam keeps going to Balak, as God knew he really wanted to go. Did he curse or bless the Israelites? He blessed them four times. He ended up doing God's will. But because Balaam disobeyed the first commandment of God, in chapter 31, verse 8, he was killed, along with the rest of the Moabites. Disobeying God enacts a high price.

It's always better to line our will up with God's in all areas of our lives. We should never bargain with God because the consequences will be dire. He loves us and only wants the best for our lives and as He can see into the future, He can clearly see what's up ahead for all of us as a result of our choices.

Let's pray:

> *Father, I thank you that You love us. Help us*
> *to do your perfect will all the time and let us*
> *not fall into the trap of questioning you. Lord,*
> *we don't want to be in your permissive will as*
> *we know the consequences are dire. We want*
> *to please you. Help us to live according to Your*
> *Word. We love you. Amen.*

The Battle of Lust

Lust is a battle we must all face sometime in our life. In the *Oxford Dictionary*, 'lust' means 'strong sexual desire'. But it can also mean a strong desire for something like food, an adrenaline rush or career progression. It's a desire that comes from a number of places.

In 1 John 2:15–16, it states:

> *Do not love the world or the things in the world.*
> *If anyone loves the world, the love of the Father*
> *is not in him. For all that is in the world—the*
> *lust of the flesh, the lust of the eyes, and the*
> *pride of life—is not of the Father but is of the*
> *world.*

As noted in the above verses, lust comes from either what we see or what we touch, sense, taste and smell. It permeates every part of our lives and takes us away from our worship and love of God.

But surely it can't be that dangerous. Let's have a look at the story in Numbers 25, starting at verse 1. This story is about Israel's harlotry with Moab.

Remember the story of Balak and Balaam? Balaam blessed Israel and didn't curse them, but let's see what happens when lust takes over.

The men of Israel, whilst camped in Acacia Grove, started to notice the women of Moab. These women became more desirable to them than the women of Israel. They saw and then they acted. This is how lust starts. It starts with the eyes and then actions follow.

They started inviting the women into their camp and they went into the women's camp. They had sexual relations with the women and when you do, you join yourself with that person.

God became angry. What was the punishment? The men who committed harlotry were to be hanged out in the sun and a plague began throughout the Israelite camp. Death was the result of lust.

But if this wasn't bad enough, one of the men (in verse 6) presented a Midianite woman in the middle of this and proceeded to take her into his tent. Everyone else was weeping and repenting of their sins, but this man had no remorse. So both he and the woman were killed. Then the plague stopped.

Is there something in our lives that we're lusting after? Is it food? Recognition? Is it a person who can fulfil our desires? God is the only one who can fulfil our needs because He created us. When we lust, we're telling God that He's not good enough for us. That's the reason the consequences are so great.

The only way to stop lust in our lives is to repent and fill our lives up with God and His ways. Read the Bible and get the Word of God in your heart, talk to God and make sure the friendships you have don't take you away from God. When we hunger for God and His ways and fill ourselves up that way, there will be no place for lust.

Do you want a husband or wife? Pray and ask God for this. Be friends with a whole group of people and go out with them. Don't be alone with just one person of the opposite sex. In God's timing, a friendship will turn into a deeper friendship, where you know that person is the one you will spend the rest of your life with. Seek God and He'll make it happen for you, if it's His will for your life. If not, God isn't mad at you, He just knows your life will be richer in Him being single.

Just remember, God's timing is not our timing, so wait patiently. Whilst you're waiting, strengthen your relationship with God. Friendship takes months and years, whilst romance generally happens in a much shorter time.

Let's pray:

> *Father, please forgive me for lusting after things or others, instead of filling myself up with You. Please help me see people the way You see them and not as objects for my pleasure. When the time is right, Father, please send a special someone along for me, if it is Your will for my life. Please help me get the Word in my heart so that I long only for you. In Jesus' name, amen.*

The Battle of Being Number One

Have you ever been in a situation where you wanted to be the leader, but you were overlooked? I have many times, starting with school sports all the way through to the workplace and in the church. There's an innate desire in some of us to be number one—the leader of the pack.

When we think of leadership, most times we think of recognition or fame. We want to be somebody who everyone knows and wants to aspire to. But most times, we only see a glimpse of who that person really is. We want to be the CEO of the company and be like that person or in their role, but too often, we don't want to do the work to get there or we possibly wouldn't even like being there. We might not like that person themselves if we knew them personally.

God doesn't want us to put people on a pedestal. That's the reason one of the commandments is to worship God and Him only. God, through the Bible, shows us who He is and that He's trustworthy and worthy of being followed.

As we are nearing the end of the Israelites' journey, we see that Moses is getting old and he needs to appoint a new leader. Who will be chosen? Is it one of the deputy leaders over one of the tribes or is it the best warrior in Israel?

It's none of these. It's Moses' assistant, Joshua. Joshua was Moses' right-hand man. He was like an executive assistant is to the CEO. He handled all of Moses' affairs and stayed close to the tabernacle. When Moses went up the mountain, it was Joshua who remained, not at the camp, but near the bottom of the mountain, waiting for Moses.

Numbers 27, starting at verse 12, is the story of Joshua being appointed as leader. But first, God speaks to Moses and tells him what his end will be. He will climb a mountain, view the Promised Land, and then die on that mountain. Take a second and imagine that. God says to us climb this mountain but you won't come down. I would be too scared to climb the mountain at all. Wouldn't you? Only my obedience to God would drive me upward.

In verse 16, Moses prays to God and asks him to set a man over the congregation, one who would be there for the people and would lead them in and out like sheep. Moses' requirements for the next leader weren't the deputies or a particular person, but one who would lead the people in humility and strength—a person who would be humble enough to obey God but strong enough to lead the people.

That doesn't sound like very good leadership criteria, does it? Where is their experience? What about negotiation skills? What about the ability to prioritise? What about the ability to be a warrior? In the Kingdom of God, none of those things matter. A leader needs to obey God and then have the strength and stamina to carry out His commands.

In verse 18, we read that Joshua was God's man for the job—a man who had the same spirit as Moses and would do God's will. This man had the task of leading the children of Israel over the Jordan and conquering the land.

Joshua was to be inaugurated in front of the whole congregation so all knew he was God's man for the job. Joshua was to stand before the priest whilst Moses laid his hands on him and commissioned him for the task ahead.

Did Joshua follow all of God's commands? Yes, he did. You can read about his leadership in the Book of Joshua. He took the people of Israel over the Jordan and they conquered many peoples before the end of Joshua's life. He was obedient to God and carried out all His commands. He was the perfect leader for the position.

If you aspire to leadership, read Joshua's story and gain some insight. He obeyed God and served the people and those are the only requirements.

Let's pray:

> *Father, I pray and repent of the times I have coveted a leadership position in any facet of my life for a selfish reason. I pray that You'll forgive me. God, I ask that you train me up for Your purpose for my life, whether in leadership or not. May I always obey You and serve others in whatever capacity You lead me. In Jesus' name, amen.*

The Battle of Making a Vow

Making a vow doesn't seem that big an issue. Who cares if we vow to do something and then later change our minds? God does—He takes it seriously. Why?

Behind a vow are truth and lies. When we make a vow, we're stating a truth, but when we don't keep it, it turns into a lie.

There's a story in the Bible that tells us of a man who made a rash vow that cost him everything, but we'll look at the law concerning vows first. This is found in Numbers 30. In verse 2, we see the truth and lie part of a vow clearly. It states:

> *If a man makes a vow to the Lord, or swears an oath to bind himself by some agreement, he shall not break his word; he shall do according to all that proceeds out of his mouth.*

A vow is a truth we speak and when we add an oath to it, we make it a double truth. The man's vow is straightforward, but not so a woman's, as we will see soon. Why? Because a woman is protected by the man, who is the authority figure in her life. We see this clearly in Ephesians 5:23:

> *For the husband is head of the wife, as also Christ is head of the church; and He is the Saviour of the body.*

A woman's authority figure is her father and when she marries, it's her husband. This is not to undermine women, but to protect them, as we'll see from the law of the vow. Women (I am one of them) are emotional and sometimes we say things we don't mean. For example, I vow that I'm going to pray five hours a day, but for a woman who has small children, this will generally probably never happen, unless God calls her to do it, for example, Susanna Wesley. The woman's intentions might be good, but the practicality of the vow isn't. This is where the protection of the authority figure comes in.

Numbers 30:3–5 talks about where a woman vows a vow whilst in her parents' home. If her father hears her say it and does nothing, it's binding, but if he disagrees, God will release her from her vow, as her father has overruled her.

Similarly, in verses 6 to 8, if a woman vows a vow whilst married and her husband hears her say it and does nothing, it stands, but if he disagrees and overrules her, then God will release her from her vow.

If a woman is a widow or divorced, any vow she makes will stand as she isn't protected by any male authority figure. It is why, as a single mum, God was my protector and took that role.

So what happens if a man makes a rash vow and doesn't think about it? We need to read the story of Jephthah in Judges 11 to find out the consequences.

Jephthah wasn't welcome in Israel as he was the son of a harlot, so his family drove him out (verse 2). But when an enemy came against Israel, the elders of Gilead went to get Jephthah. He was known as a mighty man of valour so his clan knew he was the one to help them in their troubles.

He went back to help them and in verses 30–32, he made a vow to the Lord and said:

> *"If you will indeed deliver the people of Ammon*
> *into my hands, then it will be that whatever*
> *comes out of the doors of my house to meet*

> *me, when I return in peace from the people of*
> *Ammon, shall surely be the Lord's and I will*
> *offer it up as a burnt offering."*

Let's think about this vow for a minute. How did Jephthah know what or who would come out of the doors of his house to meet him? Did he have a faithful dog that always came out before anybody or anything else? He could have added words to that vow that would have prevented what actually happened. That's why we must be careful when we make a vow and know what we're saying.

Jephthah and the men of Israel defeated the enemy in verses 32–33 and peace came to the people of Ammon. What happened to his vow? Verse 34 says that when he arrived home, his only daughter came out to meet him with timbrels and dancing. If she knew he won the battle, why didn't someone warn her to stay in the house and send something else out instead? Maybe nobody had heard the vow Jephthah had made with God.

So what happened to his daughter? She went away with her friends for two months into the mountains to mourn the future she would never have. Then Jephthah sacrificed her. This is a sad ending to a happy story of victory for the Gileadites, but it serves as a warning to us. In Ecclesiastes 5:4–5, it states:

> *When you make a vow to God, do not delay to*
> *pay it; For He has no pleasure in fools. Pay what*
> *you have vowed—Better not to vow than to*
> *vow and not pay.*

A vow seems like a good thing to do but only if we intend to carry it out. Don't make a vow rashly or the consequences could be dire. Be careful with your words. If you do make a vow, you have the opportunity to repent, but may still have to face those consequences.

In the battle of the vow, it's best not to vow. Let's pray:

> *Father, I thank you for Your Word and the stories You have in there for our safety and protection. Please help us not to vow or only to vow when we intend to carry it out. Place a watch over our mouths so what comes out is truth and not lies. Thank you for your protection of us and the hierarchy of protection you provide in the Bible. In Jesus' name, amen.*

Chapter 11—Review of Lessons Learned

The last book we will consider in our journey from Egypt to the Promised Land is the book of Deuteronomy. We'll look through this book and do a recap of the lessons learned in the previous chapters.

This is Moses' last speech to the Israelites before he dies and the Israelites cross the Jordan into the Promised Land to start their new lives. This is a life that they've never known before but all the lessons they learned in the wilderness will stand them in good stead.

A person's last words are important. I remember when my dad died; he told all of us that he loved us. I'm sure it wasn't the only time he said it, but it was so significant because he didn't tell us often. One of the grandchildren had never heard him say 'I love you' before and he was a teenager. Those memories of last words carry us through our grief and our lifetime.

Another person in the Bible whose last words were significant was Jesus. In the book of John, chapters 13 to 17 are devoted to Jesus' last words to His disciples. It was His final instructions to them. I have nearly just finished reading the book of John in a study and have been amazed at how significant those last words are.

In John 13:34, Jesus gave His disciples a new commandment to 'love one another as I have loved you'. Jesus lived this commandment in front of them for around three years but it was time for them to grab a hold of it for themselves and put it into action.

In John 14:13, Jesus tells them that if they ask anything in

His name, He will do it. This opens the door for the disciples to go directly to God for their needs and not through a priest—so significant.

My favourite is in John 17:20. The last words of Jesus are a prayer 'for all who will believe in me through their word'. Jesus' last words were for you and me. That's so significant. He prayed that we would be united in Him and God and with them so that others would know that Jesus came and of his love for them.

Can you see why last words are so significant? They not only leave us with instructions but with legacy and purpose, with a hope for our future.

Let's have an in-depth look at Moses' last words to the children of Israel and their significance.

Leave the Mountain

In Deuteronomy chapter 1 verses 2 to 8, Moses recounted the previous command to enter the Promised Land. He told them that the journey was 11 days but it took them 40 years. Then one day, God spoke and said, 'You have dwelt long enough at this mountain.'

I find it interesting that in the memories of their time in the wilderness, the first thing Moses mentioned was their refusal to enter the Promised Land the first time. Is he saying this to make them feel bad? No, he's saying this to remind them that this journey could have been much shorter.

For some of us, walking from Egypt to the Promised Land will take a short time, while for others, it may take longer. It all depends on us and our journey with God through those wilderness seasons. If it is a short lesson, then it will be shorter in the wilderness, or it could be a situation where we need to spend longer in the wilderness to put our roots in God down deeper. I have been through both in my life and the shorter one is definitely not easier than the longer one – sometimes it can be more intense.

Fear, as we have already discussed, can hold us back, but we need to be reminded daily of God's promises to us. God is saying to all of us, 'It's time to journey on. You've stayed at this mountain long enough.' Some have been on the mountain of regret, some the mountain of fear, some the mountain of laziness or maybe stuck in their minds because of something happening around them or in them. It's time to leave the mountain. We have all dwelt on it long enough.

It's time to fight some more battles so we can journey into the Promised Land. Maybe for you, the Promised Land is a career change. Maybe it's a new location or a mindset. Maybe it's time for you to walk forward in the calling and purpose God has for your life.

Will it be hard? One hundred percent yes! Will it be worth it? One hundred percent yes! So let's get off the mountain and delve into more memories that God wants to leave us with. If you find yourself in this situation let's pray together and if not, pray this for someone you know who needs it:

> *Father, I know it's time for me to come down off this mountain where I have been camped. It's time for me to walk forward into the Promised Land that you set in my life long ago. God, where I am is not where I want to be. Make me discontent with where I am so I will walk forward in what You have for me. In Jesus' name, amen.*

Appointing Authority

The next lesson God wants us to be reminded of is leadership. It's so important in every facet of our lives. Sometimes we baulk at having leaders over our lives at church, as it's just a place we go to on a Sunday, much the same as a club. But even sports clubs have presidents and coaches who lead. God sets leadership over us not to limit us, but to protect us. When you're under a good leader, you feel safe, respected and valued. If you are not currently under a good leader, seek God as to what you should do but don't be under a person who makes you feel unsafe.

God set up a leadership structure in the early Christian churches. We find this in Ephesians 4:11:

> *And he himself gave some to be apostles, some prophets, some evangelists and some pastors and teachers.*

What was the reason for these leadership positions in the church? Verse 12 tells us—'for the equipping of the saints for the work of the ministry, for the edifying of the body of Christ'. These leaders were to equip the saints (that's you and me) to go and do the work of the ministry (healing the sick, instructing others, telling others about Jesus, etc).

Then in 1 Timothy 3, Paul instructs Timothy on how to set up the leadership within each church body. There were to be bishops and deacons and they were to be men of exemplary character.

It was the same in Israel. God had appointed Moses as the leader and Aaron as his spokesman. But it was impossible for two men to meet the leadership needs of millions of people. In Deuteronomy 1:9, Moses makes this exact complaint to the people, 'I alone am not able to bear you.' So what was the solution?

He instructed the Israelites in verse 13, to 'choose wise, understanding, and knowledgeable men from among your tribes, and I will make them heads over you'. There were criteria for leadership; they couldn't choose just anyone. They had to be wise, understanding (or compassionate) and knowledgeable. They couldn't be dictators, ruffians or unwise persons.

So now the leaders are Moses, Aaron and 12 men (one from each tribe of Israel). Was that enough? No, it wasn't. In verse 15, more leaders are appointed—leaders over thousands, hundreds, fifties, tens and officers for the tribes.

Then in verses 16 and 17, the leaders were told how they were to behave and judge the cases that arose between the Israelites. They were to judge righteously and without partiality. Then if the case was too hard, they could bring it to Moses.

So why is leadership an important lesson for us to remember? First, God appoints leaders. This is found in Romans 13:1, which states:

> *For there is no authority except from God, and*
> *the authorities that exist are appointed by God.*

Does that mean the bad leaders too? That's what it says.

But do we have some responsibility for who is appointed? Yes, that's the second point. The verses for this are found in 1 Timothy 2: 1–3, which states:

> *Therefore I exhort first of all that supplications,*
> *prayers, intercession, and giving of thanks be*
> *made for all men, for kings and all who are*

> *in authority, that we may lead a quiet and*
> *peaceable life in all godliness and reverence. For*
> *this is good and acceptable in the sight of God*
> *our Saviour.*

What is our responsibility? It's to pray for all in authority over us in every facet of our lives, from our homes to our workplaces, to our schools to our governments. Why? So that we can lead a quiet and peaceable life—a life where we live in peace and have the abundant life Jesus came to give us (John 10:10).

If you're a leader, then ensure that you're leading as Jesus would—with humility, wisdom, impartiality and compassion.

Authority is important in our lives and we shouldn't scoff at it. Let's pray:

> *Father, I thank You for every leader You have*
> *appointed over my life. I thank You that each*
> *of them leads the way Jesus leads. May I be*
> *respectful to each one and pray for them so that*
> *my life will be peaceful and abundant. In Jesus'*
> *name, amen.*

Wilderness

The next memory is not a lesson but a season. Every so often in our Christian lives, we end up in a wilderness season. This isn't meant to break us but to make and mould us into who we need to be in the next season of our lives. However, some of us never advance through our wilderness season (like the original Israelites who were over 20 years old (except for Caleb and Joshua)). Whether we go through the wilderness seasons in our lives or continue to camp there is the choice of each of us individually.

In Deuteronomy 2:1–25, Moses recounts this wilderness season for the Israelites. This was the season before they started the war against different kings. A wilderness season will always precede a time of warfare. As Christians, we don't battle against flesh and blood, but against principalities, powers, rulers of darkness and spiritual hosts of wickedness (Ephesians 6:12).

The wilderness season is a season of preparation for war. This is a season where we rely on God and develop further our trust and faith in Him and His Word. Without a wilderness season, we'll never advance in the Kingdom of God.

It's also when we learn to use our armour, as set out in Ephesians 6:13–17. We learn truth, righteousness, peace, faith, salvation and how to use the Word of God in all these circumstances.

It's also a time when we learn who our enemies are. In Deuteronomy 2:4, God told Moses to tell the Israelites that they would be journeying through the territory of their brethren, the descendants of Esau. They were to watch themselves carefully and not meddle with them. They were to buy their food and water from them and not expect a handout. In the wilderness, we learn that our brethren (our fellow Christians) aren't our enemy. We are to treat each other with kindness and compassion and not 'use' each other in any way.

God did the same with the people living in the Wilderness of Moab and their land and Ammon. The Israelites weren't to battle with them because they were the descendants of Lot. In the wilderness, our enemies aren't our church family, nor are they the Church worldwide. God desires unity in His people. The wilderness is the place to learn that lesson.

Psalm 133 is a favourite of mine and verse 1 states:

> *Behold, how good and how pleasant it is for*
> *brethren to dwell together in unity.*

In verse 3 we read the result of the above verse, 'For there the Lord commanded the blessing—life forevermore.'

I'm sure all of us want to be blessed by God and have life forevermore. Therefore, we need to dwell in unity with our fellow Christians. Will we always agree? No, but unity doesn't mean sameness, it means the state of being joined as a whole. It doesn't mean agreement, it means that we acknowledge that all who believe in the death and resurrection of Jesus are our fellow Christian believers.

After the Israelites had passed their brethren's land, then in Deuteronomy 2:24, God instructs the Israelites to 'begin to possess the land and engage the king in battle'. In verse 25, it goes on to state:

> *"This day I will begin to put the dread and*
> *fear of you upon the nations under the whole*
> *heaven, who shall hear the report of you, and*
> *shall tremble and be in anguish because of you."*

When we come out of the wilderness season, we'll have a new boldness to fight and defeat our enemies. We won't be the same as when we first went in, we'll be stronger in God. The wilderness season only ends when we choose to learn the lessons of the wilderness and become strong enough in God to defeat the enemies in the next season.

We can see this in the life of Jesus. In Luke 4:1–13, Jesus was led by the Holy Spirit into the wilderness. The wilderness isn't punishment but training. Jesus was tempted by Satan for 40 days and passed all the tests. Then Satan left Him and what happened to Jesus? Verse 14 tells us that 'Jesus returned in the power of the Spirit to Galilee, and news of Him went out through all the surrounding region.'

The time Jesus spent in the wilderness prepared Him for ministry. If Jesus needed this time, then so do we. So let's not look at our wilderness seasons as being rejection from God but as preparation for the next season. Let's pray:

> *Father, I thank you for Your Word. Help us to see the wilderness seasons in our lives not as punishment but as preparation. Give us the discernment to know what season we're in and what You're trying to teach us. Help us to be open to Your leadership and guidance. In Jesus' name, amen.'*

Obedience

Obedience—none of us likes this lesson because we think that obeying God will take away our freedom. But obedience is a form of protection from God that will prevent us from being hurt from the consequences of disobedience.

This lesson is one that all parents wish their children would learn sooner. Most two-year-olds know the answer to give when their parents want them to obey. The answer is 'no'. Parents get frustrated when their children do this, but have you ever thought about what God thinks when we say a resounding 'no' to what He tells us to do?

So what is obedience? In the *Oxford Dictionary*, it means 'compliance with an order, request, or law or submission to another's authority or observance of a monastic rule'. In the first part of this definition, the word 'obedience' means obey and you won't get punished, disobey and you will. There are only two options.

In the second definition it is the observance of a monastic rule. We know that God's Kingdom has a king—Jesus. The second definition fits better with how God wants us to obey. God's command to obey is not a penance but is an observance, which is the practice of following the rules of law, morality or ritual, as defined in the *Oxford Dictionary*. It is a command that is meant to be seen and copied.

So who are we meant to be copying? Jesus. He's the reason the gospels were written. It was so we could see obedience in action.

What about the Israelites? In Deuteronomy 4, the heading is 'Moses commands obedience'. In the Old Testament, the term 'obedience' was a punishment command but this changed in the New Testament to a 'seeing and doing' command. From verses 1–14, Moses commands the children of Israel to 'listen to the statutes and the judgement which I teach you to observe' and then gives the reason for it—'that you may live and go in and possess the land which the Lord God of your fathers is giving you' (verse 1).

Let's look at some of the other commands Moses gives them in these verses:

- Verse 2—don't add to the word I commanded or take away from it

- Verse 6—observe the commands carefully
- Verse 9—take heed to yourself and diligently keep yourself lest you forget them
- Verse 9—teach them to your children and your grandchildren

What are the results of their obedience to these statutes and commandments?
- Verse 4—you are alive today because you held fast to the Lord your God
- Verse 6—you will be part of a great nation of wise and understanding people
- Verse 7—you will be part of a great nation that God is near and you can call on Him
- Verse 12—you have heard the sound of your God

God set His laws, statutes and judgements in motion in Israel so they would live long, prosperous lives. His will for us is always to live in abundance in every aspect of our lives. This happens through obedience to His Word.

Even today, in the time we're living in, God still wants us to be obedient to His Word. Why? So that we'll prosper and bring Him glory.

God's commands in the Old Testament were practical commands the Israelites could put into practice in their daily lives. The commandments to love God and love others we have been left with are sometimes harder, as our commands are to do with our heart attitude and our soul—our mind, will and emotions. But we have an advantage over the Israelites. Even though God was near to them, the Holy Spirit lives in us and can help us live the way God wants us to live.

So how about it? It's time for us, like the Israelites, to

remember that obedience isn't a punishment but a privilege. Let's pray:

> *Father, we thank you for Your Word, which helps us live the way that You want us to live. Please forgive us for those times we have been disobedient to you. Holy Spirit, speak to our hearts and direct our steps and our attitudes each day. We want to be more like Jesus, who is our example of how we should live our lives. In Jesus' name, amen.'*

Idolatry

Idolatry is our next reminder, just as it was for the Israelites. You may say, 'But Karen, we don't have idols in our homes anymore. We don't bow down to things and nor do we sacrifice to statues of animals or people.' That may be true in Western culture but in Asia and other places, idols are everywhere. They're in the temples and on the street corners. Some places have such elaborate temples to their idols and gods and the people live in poverty. This is heartbreaking to me.

If we don't have idols that we bow down to, then why should we be aware of idolatry in our lives? Let's look at what an idol is. An idol, in the *Oxford Dictionary*, is an image or representation of a god used as an object of worship. Then what is a god? I'm not going to give the dictionary definition here but my own—a god is something we worship or hold in high esteem. It could be a sport or sporting team, it could be television or it could be social media, etc. It's the thing that has such a hold on us that when God asks us to do something for Him, the 'god' prevents it.

Have you ever had God ask you to pray whilst you're scrolling through social media and you said 'soon, God'? What has the highest priority in your life and mine—God or social media? Your favourite team is playing on Sunday night but your church has planned a special night of worship. If you're struggling between sport and church, then who's your god? These are just a few examples, but you get the idea. I struggle with social media and time that I should be spending with God.

How do we break the hold of that idol in our lives? Generally by fasting from the idol and praying. Once the habit is broken, you generally don't go back to it. A few years ago, our church had a fasting and praying season at the start of the year. I felt that I should fast from television and in particular, watching the six o'clock news. I didn't watch television for three weeks, and you know what? I've hardly watched it since. I'm not sure I've ever watched the six o'clock news again. It had a hold on me and was taking up an hour of my time. Fasting broke the bonds of it in my life.

Let's look at the Israelites in Deuteronomy 4:15. In this verse, God is reminding the Israelites that when He spoke to them on the mountain, they couldn't see a form. Why? Because God didn't want them to turn him into a carved image. They would have worshipped an image of God, but not God. Let's do the same and worship God and not a man-made image of Him.

In verse 19, it starts again with similar words, 'take heed'. What does this mean? It means to listen carefully. In this verse, God warns them about looking at the creation and worshipping it instead of Him, the Creator. We need to do the same—worship God and not creation. It's great to go out into nature and do things like surfing, walking, etc, but don't put that above God.

Verse 23 is the next verse with the words 'take heed'. This time God reminds them to remember the covenant He made with them and not to make a carved image. This is one of the Ten Commandments He wants them to remember. It's the same for us—let's remember God's law to love Him always and then we won't put man-made things above Him.

For the rest of chapter four down to verse 40, God tells the Israelites who He is and what will happen if they don't remember to beware of idolatry.

The most important thing for us to remember in relation to this is to remember Who God is. He is our creator, our redeemer, our righteousness, our ever-present help, our healer, our deliverer, our friend and so much more. When we get the bigness of God deep in our hearts and minds, idolatry won't have a hold of us because we know how big our God is.

God desires our worship and wants to be number one in our lives. It's not for any reason except that He loves us and desires to have a relationship with us—His creation. That's why He sent Jesus, so we would have a person we could imitate and read about how He did life whilst He was on the earth. That's how much God loves us—He sent a part of Himself and heaven to earth. Let's pray:

> *Father, I desire for you to be number one in my life. Please show me where the idols are in my life and expose them so I can clearly see them. Help me not to hold on to those things I think are good for me, but to cling to You in everything. Please forgive me where I haven't put You in first place and help me to do better. In Jesus' name, amen.*

Choose Obedience

We get to choose obedience. This choice starts as soon as we're old enough to speak and understand speech and continues through life until we're no longer here. Obedience is always action from commands of authority. If nobody tells us what to do, there's no need for obedience.

In a democratic society like the one I live in, if I am obedient to the authority figures around me I sometimes hear comments like 'we live in freedom' or 'I don't want to' or 'this is a democracy'. Lack of obedience in societies always has a punishment. If you obey, rewards come and if you disobey, punishment comes. We generally learn this from an early age.

However, if the authority asks you to do something that is in direct opposition to the Word of God, then always choose the Word of God. For example, some countries make owning the Bible illegal but since God wants us to read His Word, then we need to obey God.

In the Old Testament, and for the Israelites, it was very much like this. In Deuteronomy 28 we read about the blessings for obedience and the curses for disobedience. The blessings are contained in 14 verses, whereas, the curses are contained in 54 verses. Blessings always come with increase and curses always come with decrease. With blessings come rewards and with curses come punishment.

In Deuteronomy 6, God warns the Israelites against disobeying. First, He tells them what He will give them when they get to the Promised Land. Those things include cities that they didn't build, houses full of good things they didn't fill, hewn-out wells they didn't dig and vineyards and olive trees they didn't plant. Can you imagine if God took you to a new city to live in and gave you a new home filled with everything you required (the furniture, the appliances, the linen, etc) and a job you didn't apply for? It would be fabulous, wouldn't it? This is what He did for the Israelites, but it came with a word of caution.

In verse 12, it states:

> *then, beware, lest you forget the Lord who brought you out of the land of Egypt, from the house of bondage.*

Beware that in all the prosperity that God gave them that they didn't forget Him and disobey. Further, the Israelites were commanded not only to obey God but to teach their family to obey Him. How? It tells us in verses 20–21 that they were to tell their children the stories of how they were brought out of Egypt. But not only tell the stories but teach how God was with them and did all those things for them because of their obedience.

In chapter 7, starting at verse 12, God tells them of the blessings of obedience as well. God tells them of the blessings of obedience so many times throughout the book of Deuteronomy because it was important that they remember that without God, there would be no blessings. God chose to bless their nation and give them a privilege over other nations. Therefore, God expected them to remember Him, His deeds and obey.

At the end of this discourse on obedience, which begins in Deuteronomy 6:10 and ends in chapter 8:20, God says in verses 19–20:

> *Then it shall be, if you by any means forget the Lord your God, and follow other gods, and*

> *serve them and worship them, I testify against*
> *you this day that you shall surely perish. As*
> *the nations which the Lord destroys before you,*
> *so you shall perish, because you would not be*
> *obedient to the voice of the Lord your God.*

This is our reminder too—don't forget God, don't follow idols, serve only God and worship Him and then blessings will follow our obedience.

So, in the New Testament, does disobedience still mean punishment? Yes, it does. Although we're not under the law, there are still spiritual laws in motion. There are still consequences for our disobedience. The only difference is that we no longer walk in the law of sin and death if we're in Christ Jesus. Romans 8:1–2 states:

> *There is therefore now no condemnation to*
> *those who are in Christ Jesus, who do not walk*
> *according to the flesh, but according to the*
> *Spirit. For the law of the Spirit of life in Christ*
> *Jesus has made me free from the law of sin and*
> *death.*

For those who have given their lives to Jesus, we walk according to the law of the Spirit of life in Christ Jesus. This means that when we disobey, we can go to Jesus and ask forgiveness and we will receive it (1 John 1:9).

So although we are under a different law, obedience to God still applies. He's the only one we worship and serve. The difference is that our walk is spiritual and theirs was natural.

Their blessings depended on their actions only, whereas our blessings depend on our walk with God and our obedience to His Word. Our thoughts and attitudes also determine our blessings. Let's determine to walk in obedience and when we sin, let's be quick to go to God. Let's pray:

> *Father, I thank You for who You are. Please help*
> *me to be obedient to Your Word as I want to live*
> *my life in blessing so I can be a blessing to others*
> *and that others can see God in me. Please forgive*
> *me for all those times when I wasn't obedient*
> *and help me to be quick to ask for forgiveness*
> *and repent. In Jesus' name, amen.*

Place of Worship

My husband and I went on a tour of Europe a number of years ago and visited many churches. We were looking at the stained glass windows and the magnificence of the buildings. After a while, however, we got tired of looking at so many old churches. We were focused on the external building, the windows and the decorations, not on the One we meet in the services.

God never meant for churches to be only buildings we tour through, but a place to meet Him. I know that God is in our houses too, but church is a place where we go to meet with God, other Christians and people who want to meet Jesus.

In Deuteronomy 12, God tells the Israelites that they must have a prescribed place of worship. Once they reached the Promised Land, they were to destroy all the places where the nations who had lived there had served their gods and destroy everything they used to serve their gods (verses 2 and 3). There was to be no reminder of the gods that had been served in those places.

Instead, in verse 5, God tells the Israelites:

> *But you shall seek the place where the Lord your God chooses, out of all your tribes, to put His name for His dwelling place, and there you shall go.*

It needed to be a designated place where they could go and serve God. They were to take their offerings there (verse 6) and eat and rejoice there (verse 7). It was to be a special place of remembrance of what God had done for them and would continue to do.

Hebrews 10:24–25 is our reminder in the New Testament to meet with others in the prescribed place of worship. Those verses state:

> *And let us consider one another in order to stir up love and good works, not forsaking the assembling of ourselves together, as is the manner of some, but exhorting one another, and so much the more as you see the Day approaching.*

So what is our reason to go to church? It tells us in these verses. It's not only to worship God but to consider others. Others need you to be in church. They need your presence. They also need your wisdom and encouragement. That is why we go—to encourage each other in the fact that we're not doing this journey alone. For me, this is a good enough reason to go to church every Sunday when I am able.

In the middle of all the verses in Deuteronomy 12 regarding the prescribed place of worship, verse 19 stands out. It states:

> *Take heed to yourself that you do not forsake the*
> *Levite as long as you live in your land.*

In God's design for the nation of Israel, the Levites were designated to look after the tabernacle, its furnishings, the offerings, etc. They were not to labour and do ordinary work but were to be dedicated to the place of worship. This meant that their provisions had to come from the offerings the people brought to the tabernacle. If the Israelites were too busy in their lives to go to the prescribed place of worship, the Levites would suffer, as they wouldn't have any provisions.

God is saying the same to you and me today. Take heed and don't forsake your pastors/priests or the leader of your church. Make sure you bring your tithes and offerings so that not only the church itself has provisions but the leader of the church will too. Sometimes, we forget that God has instructed us to do this.

Malachi 3:10 is our go-to scripture for this. It states:

> *Bring all the tithes into the storehouse, that there*
> *may be food in My house, and try Me now in this,*
> *says the Lord of hosts, if I will not open for you the*
> *windows of heaven.*

Church is where we should get our spiritual nourishment and our pastors/priests and leaders deliver this Word. That's the reason it's so important that we bless those who bless us with the Word from God. So we need to meet with God corporately in a prescribed place of worship and look after the leaders in our churches. If it's important to God, it must be important to us. Let's pray:

> *Father, I thank you that I have a church building*
> *to attend with leaders in place that You have put*
> *there and ordained. Please help me not to get so*
> *busy in my life that I don't have time to attend*
> *church with others. Allow me to bless my leaders*
> *through my tithes and offerings. In Jesus' name,*
> *amen.*

The Word of God

I like reading the Old Testament stories about the memorial stones they set up. It was their reminder that something good had happened at that place and every time they went past it, they remembered either the event or the stories behind it.

That's why memorabilia is so important to some of us. For some of us, it's looking through photos, for others it's a spoon collection or postcards, but most of us have visible reminders of our memories. These are the things we want to take with us if disaster strikes. I collect jewellery wherever I go. Most of it isn't expensive but when I wear it, it's a reminder of the places I've been.

God wanted to leave the Israelites with memories too but He also wanted to leave them with commandments written down so they could see them. For us, it's our Bibles. Our Bible tells us of the past and the stories of what God did for the people who lived long ago. It's also about our present and how we should live and about our future and the hope that we hang on to in hard times.

However, there were no printing presses when the Israelites lived. There were only stones. In Deuteronomy 27 there's a story about their Word of God and a memorial, all in one. Let's read from verses 1–3 so we can look at the story:

> *Now Moses, with the elders of Israel,*
> *commanded the people, saying: "Keep all the*
> *commandments which I command you today.*
> *And it shall be, on the day when you cross over*
> *the Jordan to the land which the Lord your God*
> *is giving you, that you shall set up for yourselves*
> *large stones, and whitewash them with lime,*
> *You shall write on them all the word of this law."*

God wanted a place where His people could go as a memorial of when they'd crossed the Jordan River but also to read the commandments He'd given them. The stones were to be whitewashed so the words could be easily read by everyone.

In verse 5, God also commanded them to build an altar there to offer burnt offerings. It was not only a place of commandments and memorials but a place of sacrifice. This is so like the Bible we have today. It's a book of commandments and memorials and tells of Jesus' ultimate sacrifice for you and me.

In this passage, we're reminded that the Bible is more than a book that sits on a shelf. It's our commandment (how we live), our memorial (how others did life and were victorious with God before us) and of sacrifice (the love God has for us in sending

His only Son to live, then die for us and then be raised so our relationship with God was restored). All we have to do now is believe.

I like sitting down with my Bible every day and learning from it. It should be a daily part of our lives so we can be more like Jesus.

Let's pray:

> *Father, I thank You that we have Your Word with us and so readily available. Please help us to treat it as just not another book but a Word directly from You. Remind us that the Word of God contains our commandments, our memorials and Your sacrifice and may we also treasure it. In Jesus' name, amen.*

The Ultimate Choice

Have you ever been shopping for clothes, electronics etc, and you had an idea of what you wanted, but there were so many choices? Do you remember the dilemma you were in? Which one did you choose and how did you choose it?

Choices—we make a multitude of choices every day, from what we eat for breakfast to what time we eat dinner at night and everything in between. We've heard the podcasts and blogs on how to make fewer choices, but it seems like life is full of them and we can't get away.

I love that God knows that about us. He knows there are so many choices to make daily that sometimes we just need someone to tell us what the best choice is. We can ask our friends or family but often their choices depend on their opinions and their likes or dislikes. Movie choices, dinner choices, career choices, house choices, furniture choices, etc, are influenced by others and often we don't like what they like.

That's why in Deuteronomy 30, starting at verse 11, God reminds the Israelites that they only have two choices. Can you imagine only having two choices in outfits, shoes, movies, food, etc? It would seem very boring after a while. However, the choices God asked the Israelites to make impacted their whole lives, not just a small portion of them. What were those two choices? I love what verses 11–13 say about them first. It states:

> *For this commandment which I command you today is not too mysterious for you, nor is it far off. It is not in heaven, that you should say, "Who will ascend into heaven for us and bring it to us, that we may hear it and do it?" Nor is it beyond the sea, that you should say "Who will go over the sea for us and bring it to us, that we may hear it and do it?"*

They weren't going to have to search for the choices, nor was it going to be hard to find them. A game of hide and seek was not in play. These choices aren't so mysterious that we won't be able to understand them or obey them. They aren't out there in the universe where we have to travel to find them. We don't need to get in a spaceship or a submarine. The choices are easy for everyone to make, no matter the age, the intellectual ability, the language or the inability to travel.

Before God tells us what these choices are, He tells us where to find them. In verse 14, it states that:

> *But the word is very near you, in your mind and*
> *in your heart, that you may do it.*

The choices are inside us. They come from our minds and our hearts and come out of our mouths. What are these mysterious choices that are part of our reminders on our journey from Egypt to the Promised Land? Verse 15–16 tells us. It states:

> *See, I have set before you today life and good,*
> *death and evil, in that I command you today*
> *to love the Lord your God, to walk in His ways,*
> *and to keep His commandments, His statutes,*
> *and His judgements, that you may live and*
> *multiply; and the Lord your God will bless you*
> *in the land which you go to possess.*

The choices are life and good or death and evil. Everything within us always wants to choose life and good but is it the life and good that God wants us to live by? Many of us think that if we live good lives, we'll go to heaven. But God's definition of good and our definition have two vastly different meanings.

God told us in the verses above his definition—to love Him, walk in His ways and keep His commandments, statutes and judgements. It's not to do our own thing or the thing that makes us happy. That won't lead to life in the end.

So does God make our choice easy? Yes, and verse 19 tells us what to choose. It states:

> *I call heaven and earth as witnesses today against you, that I have set before you life and death, blessing and cursing; therefore choose life, that both you and your descendants may live.*

What choice did God say was the best one? Life and blessing. He said that to the Israelites and He says it to us today as well. Choose life, not your kind of life, but His. One that's abundant and full of blessings. God is asking each of us to make a choice but He gives us the correct answer—choose life. Let's pray:

> *Father, I thank You that You never leave us floundering about which choice to make. You always lead us and guide us into making the best choice—the one where we love and worship You and, in turn, have an abundant life. God, we thank you that you continually remind us to choose life. In Jesus' name, amen.*

Worship

One of our last reminders from Moses is found in Deuteronomy 32, which is titled 'The Song of Moses'. This song contained some of the last words Moses spoke to the people of Israel.

Moses didn't sing this song, he spoke it. Worship isn't

always a song or even some sort of music; it's a cry of our hearts in adoration and praise of God. There's something so beautiful when we open our mouths and worship God.

In the first four verses of this song, he speaks about how good God is and how great He is and that He is 'a God of truth and without injustice; righteous and upright is He'.

This reminds me of the start of the Lord's prayer in Matthew 6, where it states:

> *"Our Father in heaven, hallowed be Your Name,*
> *Your kingdom come, Your will be done on earth*
> *as it is in heaven."*

Our worship of God needs to be centred on Him. He's the only one who sustains us, heals us, saves us, delivers us, gives us peace and so forth. He is worthy to be praised.

Then the song of Moses goes back to their history, starting in verse 5. Back before Abram was called out of Haran to go to the place that God called him (an unnamed place, as God said 'follow' and didn't say where).

It's good to remember our history with God, the times He answered our prayers, healed us or protected us in some way. That should form part of our worship too. We shouldn't dwell on the bad memories, only those good memories we have. When you lose someone close to you, these memories are what sustain you. Every birthday, every anniversary, instead of mourning, it's good to remind ourselves of the person they were or the good memories we shared with them, or even memories of the stories they told.

In verse 15, the song takes a major turn. The next few verses talk about the Israelites rejecting God and going after other idols and their own ways. Some would say this isn't worship and maybe it isn't. It could be that our worship should include what would happen if we walked away from God as this reminds us of how mighty and good He is.

These verses aren't to bring shame to the Israelites, as they were verses pertaining to future actions. However, they learned the words and sang them as a reminder or as a warning. God doesn't give us warnings because He doesn't like us. He loves us dearly and doesn't want us to fall into the traps of self and self-serving. If we keep our hearts in a worship mindset toward God, it keeps us from stumbling.

The last part of the song is about the judgement of God on the Israelites and also on their enemies. God will always judge our sin. Even though we repent, there are consequences. Our spirits are right with God but there's still a world out there.

Are these verses worship? Worship is not only a slow song and a time of meditation, it's also warfare. The last part of this song is warfare worship. It's the worship that comes upon us when we're fighting in the Spirit for something. It's a time of singing that tells the enemy we mean business.

Jehoshaphat is the best example of this in 2 Chronicles 20. A great army was coming against the Israelites so Jehoshaphat, who was the king, and all the Israelites sought the Lord about what they should do. God told them to go down and meet this great multitude the next day.

In verse 21, when the king consulted with the people, he appointed the singers and worshippers to lead the army. These people had no weapons, only their mouths of praise. Their praise was warfare praise that moved God and defeated the great army:

> *And when he consulted with the people, he appointed those who should sing to the Lord, and who should praise the beauty of holiness, as they went out before the army and were saying: "Praise the Lord, For His mercy endures forever."*

I can guarantee you that they probably weren't singing in a quiet voice or slowly, but were shouting it in warfare. They were leading the army and needed to be strong in God.

So how do we worship? We worship with adoration to God, then remembrance of the good things He's done for us, then repenting of our sin and then going into warfare on behalf of others and ourselves. It sounds similar to prayer and it is. Worship is how we lead our lives—in reverence and awe of God. Let's pray:

> *Father, I thank you that I have the privilege of worshipping You. I thank You for all You have done for me and continue to do for me. I repent of my sins and I warfare on behalf of others and myself. Thank you that my life is lived in total worship of You. In Jesus' name, amen.*

Last Words

It's now time to consider the last words Moses spoke before he died.

Before we look at the blessing, we'll consider the last words he spoke generally. They're found in Deuteronomy 32:46–47 and state:

> *"Set your hearts on all the words which I testify among you today, which you shall command your children to be careful to observe—all the words of this law. For it is not a futile thing for you, because it is your life, and by this word you shall prolong your days in the land which you cross over the Jordan to possess."*

Those words—set your heart—are the foundation for these last words. If you set your heart on something, it means you have the determination, the courage and the fight to see it through to the end. God wants the Israelites to have this same tenacity so He tells them to set their hearts.

As Christians, we need to ponder on what we set our hearts on. Is it the things of the world, our career, our money, our family, our status, etc, or is it the Word of God? In Matthew 6:33, Jesus reminds us to seek first the Kingdom of God or, in other words, to set our hearts on finding out what the Kingdom of God is and how we operate in it.

The Israelites were to set their hearts on all the words Moses spoke to them that day. Why? It tells us in verse 47, because 'it is your life'. These words and their obedience would allow them to live their lives in abundance, the way that God wanted them to.

Did God want them to live this way because He wanted to stifle their fun? No, He wanted them to enjoy life in the world He had created for them. Following these words would allow them to do this.

Last words should always have an element of generations and the words here are no exception. They were to teach them to their children and command them to observe them. These words were a generational way of life. It didn't matter where they went or if they found new ways of doing things, these words would sustain them and be their foundation in everything.

The same goes for us, as Jesus left last words for us to follow. More than that, over the centuries before that, the Word of God was put into a book so that all could read it, understand it and live their lives accordingly. The principles and foundations in the Bible don't change—they're eternal and still apply to us today. Also, they still work the same. The world around us might have changed, but the Word of God never changes.

In chapter 33, we read the blessing of Moses on Israel. Being blessed was an important cultural principle that's rare in the western world of today. Receiving the blessing of your father or your spiritual head was so important that when Jacob stole Esau's blessing, Esau became extremely upset. Blessings empowered a person so they could prosper. In essence, the last blessing speaks prosperity over future generations.

As we read through chapter 33, we see some of these blessings:

1. Reuben—his tribe would live and not die and his men would be numerous.

2. Judah—he would have sufficiency and God would help

the tribe against their enemies.

3. Levi—God would bless their substance and accept the work of their hands and would strike down those who rose against them.

4. Benjamin—the tribe would dwell in safety and God would shelter them.

5. Joseph (Ephraim and Manasseh)—the blessing would be on their land and would produce precious things and their strength would push peoples to the end of the earth.

6. Zebulun and Issachar—their tribes would enjoy the abundance of the seas and the treasures hidden in the sand.

7. Gad—the tribe would be enlarged and administer the justice of God.

8. Dan—the tribe would be a lion's offspring, meaning it would grow in strength.

9. Naphtali—the favour and blessing of God would abound.

10. Asher—blessed and favoured by the other tribes.

The tribe of Simeon is missing from the blessing. What's the reason for this? I'm unsure. In the last blessing given to the tribes (sons) by their father Jacob on his deathbed, Simeon and Levi were grouped together and were given a harsh blessing. However, the actions of Moses' mother in standing up against the Egyptian law may have overridden this harsh blessing given to the tribe of Levi, as this was the tribe of Moses and Aaron.

Whatever the reason, last words, including blessings, are important in the Bible and foretell, or prophesy, the future of the person or tribes involved.

Let's remember the power of our words because some of them are the last we will speak to a person. We may never see them again for whatever reason, so remember that the words we leave people with are powerful. Let's pray:

> *Father, I ask that You help me with the words*
> *I speak. I want blessings to come out of my*
> *mouth, not curses, as the words I speak to*
> *someone may be the last words I ever speak to*
> *them. May my words be full of grace and truth.*
> *In Jesus' name, amen.*

Chapter 12—The Jordan River

We're reaching the part of our journey where we're just about to cross the Jordan River into the Promised Land. Over the last few chapters, we've learnt a lot about what it means to live a godly life and how to do it, as we've followed the Israelites on their journey for the last 40 years.

I know in the past, I have dwelt on the length of time it took the Israelites to make that journey—an 11-day journey turned into 40 years. Would they have been ready for the Promised Land any earlier? Maybe or maybe not! The Israelites (except for Joshua and Caleb) over the age of twenty years old were obviously not ready as they continually disobeyed God and died in the wilderness.

But what about their children! I believe that if they hadn't gone through the wilderness season, then they wouldn't have been as equipped either and God would have had to teach them all these lessons once they were in the Promised Land.

It's easier to learn the lesson in the wilderness when all we have to rely on is God than it is in the Promised Land, where all our needs are met. We have seen over and over in the book of Deuteronomy where God says 'don't forget me when you come into the Promised Land'. I believe God is saying the same thing to us today—don't forget me. There is still more of me (God) to learn and there's still more I want to teach you. The wilderness is for teaching and the Promised Land is for putting the teaching into practice and celebrating the good things of God.

As we come to the Jordan River, what are our expectations of where the journey will lead us now? Is it full of hope for the future or are you weary of all the battles you may have to face? Are you celebrating this moment of arrival at a pivotal point in the journey or are you still focused on the journey ahead?

I preached a communion message a few years ago on the importance of the word 'last'. As we come to the Jordan River, I think we should consider this word. This was supposedly the last time most of the Israelites would stand on that side of the Jordan River. It was definitely close to the last time they would eat manna before they partook of the produce of the land. What became of the rock that followed them to provide for their water needs? Did this rock miraculously cease to provide? Maybe it did.

It's important to remember those last things in our lives because what comes directly after a last is always a first. The Israelites were going to embark on a completely new first once they crossed the Jordan River. After many years, they would be able to live in houses and not have to move. They could pasture their flocks and grow their own food. They would need to make their own clothes and shoes again as through the wilderness, their clothes and shoes didn't wear out (isn't this a crazy thought, that babies' clothes and shoes must have just grown with them).

The tabernacle would be in the one place where they could go and sacrifice and nobody would have to pack it up and down. No longer would they camp in the shape of a cross, but each tribe would be given their own land to tend and keep. Their way of life after 40 years on the move was changing drastically.

For 40 years, the Israelites had been reliant on God for everything. Now they were being called to go forth and obey the commands He had given them.

Can you relate to any of this? I can. When I was a new

Christian, my prayers were answered and my needs were met. But a day came when God expected me to take His Word as the truth and start to apply it to my own life. The journey of Christianity became tougher, but it also became more rewarding. No longer was I fed the milk of the Word of God, but He entrusted me with the meat of the Word. No longer did I have to be taught, now I was able to teach.

Has my obedience level or trust in God waned through this time? No. If anything, it has become stronger, as I have seen His Word work in my trials and I have come out stronger in faith and trust in God.

To continue the story of the Israelites, we need to look at Joshua 1. Before they could cross the Jordan River, God had to make sure their new leader, Joshua, had the tools he needed to ensure that God's will would be done.

New Leader

In verse 2 of Joshua 1, God makes this statement:

> *"Moses My servant is dead. Now therefore, arise, go over this Jordan, you and all this people, to the land which I am giving them— the children of Israel."*

This side of the Jordan River marked a new leadership for the children of Israel. Moses had led them for 40 years and had died. Now a new leader was to take the Israelites further. God had to make that abundantly clear to Joshua. No longer was Joshua the servant of Moses. Instead, he took on the role of leader. He was required to answer to God and not Moses and was to be led by God and not Moses.

When a change happens in our lives, some of the time it leads to a new leadership role. For example, when we're single and become married, the leadership over a man's and woman's life ceases to be their parents. Now the man must take up the leadership position in the family under God. Similarly, the woman must change the leader of her family from dad to husband.

Sometimes new seasons mean job changes or church changes or even family changes. The change of seasons isn't meant to break us but to take us forward in the new Promised Land that God has for us.

Promises and Requirements

Verse 3 of Joshua 1 tells Joshua what to do. It says:

> *Every place that the sole of your foot will tread upon I have given you, as I said to Moses.*

The Promised Land isn't to be looked at and admired, but to be conquered and taken. Wherever Joshua walked in that land was the inheritance for him and the children of Israel. In new seasons, we must spiritually walk over the ground God has given us and claim it. It's a good land because God has given it to us and allowed us to cross the Jordan River to get to it. Verse 4 tells Joshua all the land that he needs to possess.

I really like verse 5, as it gives Joshua and the Israelites assurance that God would be with them and would protect them. It states:

> *No man shall be able to stand before you all the days of your life; as I was with Moses, so I will be*

with you. I will not leave you nor forsake you.

This promise holds so much truth as we venture into our own Promised Land with God. It's a verse we can stand on daily in our walk with God through the things happening around us. We don't need to fear because God is with us. This is one of the sweetest promises we will hear.

But God gave Joshua a bonus. Joshua had walked the journey with Moses from the time he'd left Egypt until the time Moses died. Joshua had been his right-hand man. He saw how God was with Moses and saw the strategies Moses, through God, put in place for provision, walking through the wilderness and fighting the battles they'd faced. Joshua not only knew the stories, he experienced them.

The Bible is to us what Moses was to Joshua. It's our guarantee. In its pages, we read about how God helped others overcome obstacles. He'll do the same for us. The promise 'God will never leave us nor forsake us' is as true today as it was then and will forever be. God is trustworthy and His promises are yes and amen.

Verses 6–9 are our response to the previous verses. In each step of our Christian walk, there's always a promise and a response. These verses are Joshua's responsibility. They are his commands from God to obey in order that the previous promises come to pass. God doesn't want us nor does He expect us to sit idly by and wait for things to come to pass in our lives. We're to be active in believing and seeing in the spiritual at all times.

But what about the verse in Isaiah that says 'wait on the Lord'. Waiting there isn't an idle word, it's an active word. It means to sit on the edge of your seat and wait expectantly for something. God isn't in the business of laziness but of active faith and trust.

Let's summarise what these verses require:

- Be strong and of good courage. Don't let fear rob us of taking our Promised Land. Our inheritances awaits on the other side of our courage.
- Be strong and very courageous. Follow the laws of God and be obedient to them and then we will prosper in our ways. This still applies today—follow God and His ways and you will prosper and have an abundant life.
- The Book of the Law shall not depart from your mouth. God's Words must be forever on our lips and we must respond to every situation with the Word of God and not fear and doubt. This is hard to do, but as we practice, it will become second nature. But first, read the Bible and get to know what it says.
- Be strong and of good courage. Why? Because God is with us wherever we go. He will never leave us nor forsake us.

Do these verses require a good education, a good upbringing, that we're perfect in our ways, handsome or pretty? No! They require us to be strong in God and courageous so we can follow where He leads us, with the Word of God as our backup. This means that anyone can cross the Jordan and get to their Promised Land, whether young or old, etc. The only thing that matters to God is that we obey Him and have courage.

Preparation

Joshua 1:11 onwards talks about the preparation that went into crossing the Jordan. God didn't miraculously place them in the Promised Land. There was a preparation period that needed to take place.

The first thing they needed to do was prepare provisions. We need to make sure that we're ready to go in and take our Promised Land. Are we filled up with the Word of God? Have we sought the strategy through prayer? Is it the right timing to go in?

The second thing was that someone needed to go and spy out the land, especially the first city to conquer. Did it have big walls? What were the people like? Were there a lot of them and what were they saying about the Israelites?

This is similar to the story of Gideon in Judges (Judges 7:9). God told Gideon to go down and fight the Midianites, who were oppressing Israel at that time. When only 300 men were selected, Gideon was afraid. God knew it and told him to go down into the camp in the middle of the night and take Purah, his servant. They were to listen to what the Midianites were saying.

When they snuck into the camp, Gideon heard one man telling another a dream that he'd had. In verse 14, the interpretation of that dream was 'this is nothing else but the sword of Gideon ... Into his hand, God has delivered Midian and the whole camp'. What an interpretation! Gideon was no longer afraid, as God was on his side.

Joshua felt the same way many years before. He had been one of the 12 spies in the Promised Land some 40 years before. He desperately wanted to go back to the place he had already seen but what was the atmosphere like by this time?

In Joshua 2, Joshua sends two men in and they come to the house of Rahab the harlot in Jericho. She hid the two men from the king and then made this amazing statement in verses 9–11:

> *"I know that the Lord has given you the land, that the terror of you has fallen on us, and that all the inhabitants of the land are fainthearted because of you. For we have heard how the Lord dried up the water of the Red Sea for you when you came out of Egypt, and what you did to the two kings of the Amorites who were on the other side of the Jordan, Sihon and Og, whom you utterly destroyed. And as soon as we heard these things, our hearts melted; neither did there remain any more courage in anyone because of you, for the Lord your God, He is God in heaven above and on earth beneath."*

Hang on, these people who lived in the Promised Land had been scared of the Israelites since they came out of Egypt 40 years earlier. The Israelites had thought they appeared as grasshoppers in these people's eyes, but they didn't, they were people with a mighty God on their side.

When the men came back to the Israelite camp, they told Joshua this and much more of what had befallen them. But their report was so different from the report from many years earlier. Their report was (in verse 24):

> *And they said to Joshua, "Truly the Lord has delivered all the land into our hands, for indeed*

> *all the inhabitants of the country are fainthearted
> because of us."*

This was such a different report, but it spurred the Israelites into action to cross the Jordan to take their Promised Land.

This is the same for you and me. God goes before us in every situation we come across. If we just trust in Him, we can be the same as these two spies. God has already delivered us so let's go in and conquer the land.

Parade

In nearly every war situation we see in the movies or on television, the troops march out. Its how you go in that affects the outcome. If you go into war with your head down looking defeated, you will be defeated. But if you march together in formation, with your heads held high and arms by your side, you're more likely to conquer and be courageous.

This was the same as the parade that happened when the Israelites crossed the Jordan River. It wasn't a jumble, it was well-ordered and well-structured.

The first thing to note in Joshua 3:1 is that Joshua rose early in the morning. The Israelites got an early start when they headed from Acacia Grove to the Jordan River. I wonder why this is. I don't know about you, but morning is my best time—I get a lot done in the morning and fade in the afternoon. The early morning is also not as hot so it would have been cooler.

Once they arrived at the Jordan River, they stayed there for three days to get organised.

Let's look at the parade that went across:
1. The Ark of the Covenant of the Lord went first with the priests and the Levites bearing it. This ark held

the Ten Commandments (the Word of God), Aaron's rod that budded (the authority of God) and the manna (the provision of God). It was those things that led the people across the Jordan River.

2. Next came the people 2000 cubits (or about 900 metres) behind the ark.

But then a strange thing happened. Once the first priests' feet dipped in the edge of the water, the Jordan River parted (verse 15). The priests bearing the ark went halfway and stayed there until all the people had crossed. The ark must have become heavy after a time or God supernaturally gave them the strength to keep holding it.

One man from every tribe was also selected to pick up a stone from the place where the priests stood and carry it to the place where they were to lodge that night for a memorial for future generations.

Once the people were across, the priests bearing the Ark of the Covenant also continued across. When the soles of their feet touched dry land, the waters of the Jordan returned and overflowed all its banks as before (chapter 4:18).

The crossing of the Jordan was complete and the Israelites had finally reached the Promised Land.

Let's pray:

> *Father, I thank You that your Word is true and that You have a Promised Land for each of us to go into. I thank You that through this book, You have prepared us and given us promises we can cling to as we walk through life. I thank You that we have grown closer to You and understand the love and kindness of God even more. Amen.*

Epilogue

What was in this Promised Land that was so important and how does it relate to our lives today? The Promised Land for the Israelites, represented the fulfilment of the promise of God made many years before. It should have cemented in their minds that God's Word was true, unchanging and could forever be trusted. But it wasn't like that for them, and probably won't be for us.

The steps that the Israelites took in getting to the Promised Land, as outlined in the earlier chapters of this book, need to be kept on a daily, weekly, monthly, yearly basis. They need to be at the forefront of our minds continually.

We will all have those days when things don't go right and we have to ensure we are embedded in the Word of God so that our first thoughts are of what God would say and do. Is it easy? No, but it's worth it.

As New Testament Christians, does the Old Testament really matter? Yes, a thousand times, yes. The Old Testament is the natural principles of God in action over many thousands of years. What we're taught in the New Testament is worked out in the Old Testament by people just like you and me.

However, we have an advantage that they didn't have. We have Jesus, who showed us how to live on earth, then died on the cross for us and rose again so we can have access directly to God to hear what He's saying to us. We don't have to wait for a prophet or great leader, we have been given the access, if we believe in Jesus and that He died on the cross and rose again, and that it was directly for you and me.

After Jesus rose from the dead and ascended back into

heaven, God sent His Spirit to dwell within us, the same Spirit that hovered over the earth on creation. This is phenomenal to think about—God now lives within us and everything Jesus came to die for is ours as an inheritance.

What is that inheritance? It's the same as it was for the Israelites, only better. Every one of God's promises in the Word of God is for us individually. If the Bible says we're blessed, we're blessed. If it says we're the righteousness of God in Christ Jesus (have right standing with God), then we do. If the Bible says that God wants to prosper us, spirit, soul and body, then He does.

The only difference is that with God dwelling inside us, there's a force that we can access more readily, and that's the force of faith. Faith is believing in God and trusting that His Word is true before we see it in the natural. If we don't have faith, none of the promises in the Word of God will come true for us individually. We may see miracles at church through someone else's faith but it won't be through our own unless we unmistakably believe the Word of God.

I will conclude with Hebrews 9:15:

> *And for this reason He is the Mediator of the new covenant, by means of death, for the redemption of transgressions under the first covenant, that those who are called may receive the promise of the eternal inheritance.*

The Israelites lived under the first covenant and received the inheritance of a physical Promised Land. We live under the second covenant and have an inheritance on this earth of every promise in the Word of God and in eternity, the hope that we'll be with Jesus forever.

About the author

Karen is passionate about seeing people live their lives the way God intended and to fulfil the purpose and plans that God has for them.

She has run a number of life groups and taught teen church and Sunday school. She loves ministering to others one on one.

She resides in Australia with her husband and has two adult sons and three adult step daughters.

Continue your spiritual journey
www.livingthelifegodintended.com

www.ingramcontent.com/pod-product-compliance
Lightning Source LLC
Chambersburg PA
CBHW030255010526
44107CB00053B/1729